Outsource Your Mobile App Business

Ethics and Pragmatics of Hiring Genius Software Developers Worldwide

GREG WIENTJES, PhD

Outsource Your Mobile App Business

Available for purchase on Amazon, the Kindle and iPad iBookstore.

Also by the author:

Creative Genius In Technology: Mentor Principles from Life Stories of Geniuses and Visionaries of the Singularity

http://www.amazon.com/dp/146372750X/
http://www.geniustory.com
https://itunes.apple.com/us/book/creative-genius-in-technology/
id455574017?mt=11

iPhone Programming Screencasts: The Fastest Way to Learn iPhone Programming. Guaranteed.

http://amzn.com/B00C49T4Z2

Outsourcing as a Super Power

Do you dream of changing the world? Do you envision yourself as a 'Change Agent' that will positively impact the lives of millions or even billions of people worldwide?

I wrote this book as a 'How To' manual for outsourcing (the 'pragmatics')—teaching you to recruit, retain and collaborate together with genius computer software developers available to you worldwide. Your collaborations with these genius software programmers will literally give you "super powers". [1] [2] You will be smarter; you will have greater knowledge; you will be able to computer program—vicariously; you will be able to materialize your visions and designs into real software—launching your apps into the 'wild' among the 2.1 billion+ smartphones out in the world.

With outsourcing, you won't have to spend years in training learning how to write computer code. You won't have to raise millions of dollars from investors to hire $100k+ per year programmers based locally. Outsourcing feels a bit like "cheating" at times: you get the benefits and productivity of genius software developers around the world, and you didn't have to put in the years of toil doing homework, studying at school and learning the code. You will be able to hire software developers—just from your own personal savings—and work together with these geniuses online to build your apps and make your dreams a reality!

This book is written for the students at Singularity University Graduate Studies Program (GSP). Singularity University—cofounded by Ray Kurzweil and Peter Diamandis—admitted each class of GSP students with the intent of empowering them to harness the capabilities of exponential technologies to improve the lives of one billion or more people. GSP students are trained to help people in the areas of worldwide 'Grand Challenges', including global health, environment, prosperity, energy, space, food, water, security, education, disasters, and governance.

I gave lectures at Singularity University (SU) each summer over the past four years in the Networks and Computing track on the topic that this book centers on: Outsourcing a mobile app business. Additionally, I was member of the first GSP class in 2009.

---

[1] Lacity, M. C., & Willcocks, L. (2000). Global information technology outsourcing: In search of business advantage. John Wiley & Sons, Inc..

[2] Quinn, J. B., & Strategy, E. S. (2013). Strategic outsourcing: leveraging knowledge capabilities. Image, 34.

After my presentation this year, July 2015, I felt the time came for me to transform my presentation information into a book, a coherent set of techniques and resources for SU students to take away with them as they journey ahead towards their mission of improving the lives of one billion people. In this book, I outline the "nuts and bolts" of outsourcing. I offer you effective methods and techniques that I personally developed in my experience starting and growing an Internet-centered mobile application business. These methods for outsourcing will accelerate your 'learning curve' for finding talented software developers and help you to get the results you want, while simultaneously keeping your costs to an affordable, sustainable level.

I felt surprised, this year, to see some members of the GSP class conflicted by the ethics of outsourcing. On one hand, six or so students came to me after my talk, expressing their enthusiasm. They expressed excitement about the new tools and resources for software development they suddenly had access to through outsourcing. On the other hand, some students voiced questions about the ethics of outsourcing. These questions centered on whether outsourcing adequately benefited 'both sides'—the providers, as well as the 'consumers' of the outsourcing products. Some suggested that outsourcing might be a 'Lose-Win' relationship, where the providers of the outsource labor did not sufficiently benefit by the interaction. I, personally, view outsourcing as mutually beneficial to both parties—the providers, as well as the consumers—and I argue, in this book, that the relationship is a "Win-Win" situation. I address the ethical questions that the SU students this year introduced to me in the Question and Answer session held after my presentation.

I would furthermore like to add that the outsourcing techniques I present here also apply more generally to recruiting a vast team of talented and affordable individuals (your "virtual team") with a wide range of skills beyond computer programming, nearly every aspect of a mobile app business. These individuals can contribute to your business in areas as broad as customer support, sales, administrative tasks, data entry, accounting, personal assistance, virtual assistance, and recruitment—as well as software development.

The cost savings of outsourcing—in addition to access to computer software engineering talent that you wouldn't have access to locally—are the primary motivations for learning this approach to starting and running a business. For example, suppose you hire 15 Full-Time Filipinos at $250 per month to operate your mobile, Internet-based business. $250 per month is very much a "market rate" salary for local jobs based in the Philippines—"market rate" even for university graduates. $250 per month is a "good living" for families in the Philippines, particularly in the province, outside of densely populated urban areas. Unemployment in the Philippines is sky high. This team of 15 Full-Time workers (40 hours per week) would cost you $3,750 per month—that's $45,000 per year. Even if you needed to pay programmers a bit more, e.g., $400-500 per month, your costs to support the team are still within the budget of many people's personal savings.

Meanwhile, in contrast, suppose you hired university graduates back in good old USA and paid them a modest $70,000 per year. That adds up to $1,050,000 per year for a team of 15 people. Now you're stuck raising $3 million from investors in order to have three years ahead of you to operate the business. This assumes you'll even be able to persuade such investors, as well as tolerate partial ownership and control relinquishment and put up with all their questions and critiques.

Of course, many entrepreneurs don't need to hire 15 Full-Time workers right from the start. Just one to three workers might be sufficient to build your first prototype software, verify demand for your product in the market, and make your first few sales to customers. You can literally get your business "off the ground" with just $500-$1000 per month (Christmas gift cash) by hiring outsourced developers, or even less if you do "fixed project" contracts with developers.

Just on a personal note, that's how I got started with mobile app outsourcing. I finished my PhD from Stanford University in 2010. I had very little money and a mountain of student loan debt from graduate school. I moved in with my parents in their small California apartment and lived in a small room at their place for a year. In that humble circumstance, I led a team of 7 outsourcing workers on Skype Video chat (whom I recruited through oDesk.com / UpWork.com) and experimented with my software and product offerings. With my outsourced virtual team, I finally reached the point of making sales and helped 10s of thousands of users with my website and mobile app business.

That's how you've got to do it! Keep your costs very low in the beginning. You will make mistakes. You want to make "low cost mistakes" and learn from them. Running out of cash is the point when your business dies and your dream vanishes. With a low cash 'burn-rate', keep experimenting until you discover "product-market fit" and catch that "exponential wave" to pull your business up from near-death and into financial success and positive impact on the world.

Now you have a taste of what's possible when you get really good at outsourcing!

I am excited to see the amazing mobile apps that you—the students of Singularity University GSP—will create with the skills and knowledge that you gain from my book.

Now let's get started on learning specific techniques and resources to outsource your mobile app business!

Sincerely,
Greg Wientjes, PhD
Stanford, California. July 12, 2015

Contents

Ethics: Outsourcing As A "Win-Win" Strategy

Income 4
Experience 5
Credentials 5
Networking 5
Mentoring...5
Making A Difference...6

Introduction

Why Build Mobile App Software? 8
Instagram's Story Of Exponential Growth.......................................11
If You Can't Code, Hire Coders...14
Exoskeleton—Outsourcing Super Powers.......................................15
Take Baby Steps—A Cautionary Tale 17

Funnel Hiring

How Funnel Hiring Works...19
Recruiting Your Developers..22

People Supply

Where Do I Like To Find My Workers?..27
Broader Networks Of Available Outsourcing Workers.....................28
Full-Time Filipinos 29
Worker Profiles On Outsourcing Websites 32
Getting Candidate Workers: Sending Invitations And Posting Jobs...........39
Employment Contracts On Upwork.Com...40
Funnel Hiring In Action 42

Performance Tests

Designing Your Performance Tests: Detailed Mockups 46
Speed Up Your Testing: Web Forms For Candidates' Submissions 47
Rapid Evaluation And Advancement Of Candidates—Pass/Fail Tests 49
Discover The Genius Developer...50

Communication And Collaboration

Skype Video Chat With Your Team 53
Create A "Hive Mind" Team Using Slack Messaging 54
Regular Meetings With Gotomeeting And 'Synergy Reports'...................55
Visiting Your Team Physically In Their Country..........................57

Example

Building A Mobile App For My Marketplace Business 61
Mockup Sketches Of My Envisioned Mobile App Using Gomockingbird....
    61
Simulating Your App Using Appcooker 62
'Storyboard' Screens Of Your App Using Appcooker 66
Creation Tools For Your Simulated App Using Appcooker........................67
A Functional App 68
My Genius Developer: Amdad 69

Summary Of Resources

People Supply 71
Tools For Your Outsourcing..72

You Can Do It

Acknowledgements

Ethics: Outsourcing As A "Win-Win" Strategy

In my presentation to the GSP class this year, I emphasized outsourcing's benefits to consumers of such services, and yet I did not highlight the benefits to providers of these services. I suggest that outsourcing is a "win-win" strategy for both the providers as well as the consumers of the outsourcing products. I note some of outsourcing's benefits to providers later in this section.

Some students from the GSP this year introduced concerns about the ethics of outsourcing and the techniques that I describe in this book. I would like to acknowledge these concerns and affirm the validity of these questions about ethics. Some GSP students voiced ethics concerns about:

- Outsourcing as a form of "Neocolonialism". [3]
- Outsourcing as an exploitation of vulnerable people in developing nations—the "Precariat" class that emerged from the entrenchment of neoliberal capitalism; people that lack job security and live a precarious existence. [4] [5]
- Comments about outsourcing work performed by specific nationalities ("Filipinos") and associated evaluative statements about cultures as "over generalizations" and stereotypes. [6] [7]
- Outsourcing methods described in this book as a practice of paternalism. [8] [9]
- Outsourcing methods described in this book as a practice of "commoditizing people" and—regarding their labor as tools—without

---

[3] Sartre, J. P. (2001). Colonialism and neocolonialism. Psychology Press.

[4] Johnson, C. G. (2011). The Urban Precariat, Neoliberalization, and the Soft Power of Humanitarian Design. Journal of Developing Societies, 27(3-4), 445-475.

[5] Standing, G. (2014). The Precariat-The new dangerous class. Amalgam-časopis studenata sociologije, 6(6-7), 115-119.

[6] Steele, C. M., Spencer, S. J., & Aronson, J. (2002). Contending with group image: The psychology of stereotype and social identity threat. Advances in experimental social psychology, 34, 379-440.

[7] Blaut, J. M. (1992). The theory of cultural racism. Antipode, 24(4), 289-299.

[8] Mead, L. M. (1997). The new paternalism: Supervisory approaches to poverty. Jessica Kingsley Publishers.

[9] Thaler, R. H., & Sunstein, C. R. (2003). Libertarian paternalism. American Economic Review, 175-179.

sufficient respect for inherent human dignity, personal autonomy and worth. [10] [11] [12]

• Outsourcing methods described in this book unfairly "tilt the advantage" to the employer, leading to workers' salaries as lower than deserved. [13]

I don't have the "answers" to these ethical questions, and I respect these concerns. I also respect you if you believe outsourcing is not ethical. However, I believe outsourcing is a "win-win" strategy—a mutually beneficial practice—and outsourcing will make you highly effective in achieving success in your mobile app business.

I can tell you that I share the concerns discussed above, and I also have questions about ethics—a number of these topics occurred to me in the past. I personally feel concerns associated with Western civilization's legacy of slavery[14], colonialism, neocolonialism, sweat shops[15], illegitimate odious debt-infliction on developing nations[16], and multinational corporations' victimization of vulnerable populations.[17] [18]

From my standpoint, as a Singularity University GSP alumni, I want to help improve the lives of people—people living in my own country and abroad. I discovered outsourcing because I needed help with my

---

[10] Fuchs, C. (2010). Labor in Informational Capitalism and on the Internet. The Information Society, 26(3), 179-196.

[11] Scholz, T. (Ed.). (2012). Digital labor: The internet as playground and factory. Routledge.

[12] Doh, J. P. (2005). Offshore outsourcing: implications for international business and strategic management theory and practice. Journal of Management Studies, 42(3), 695-704.

[13] Fisher, R., Ury, W. L., & Patton, B. (2011). Getting to yes: Negotiating agreement without giving in. Penguin.

[14] Williams, E. (1994). Capitalism and slavery. UNC Press Books.

[15] Esbenshade, J. L. (2009). Monitoring sweatshops: Workers, consumers, and the global apparel industry. Temple University Press.

[16] Kremer, M., & Jayachandran, S. (2002). Odious debt (No. w8953). National Bureau of Economic Research.

[17] Agyeman, J. (2003). Just sustainabilities: development in an unequal world. MIT Press.

[18] Sachs, J. (2006). The end of poverty: economic possibilities for our time. Penguin.

programming skills, as well as getting help with the business I'm trying to run.

I'm sharing my advice about outsourcing to you because I believe this method can assist you in your 'Grand Challenge' GSP team project and life beyond, as a Singularity University graduate. I am not looking to perpetuate neocolonialism, multinational corporate hegemony or cultural racism.

I'm trying to do my best to help people through the products and services that I offer in my business. I also want to assist the team of people I work with—mainly outsourcing workers overseas in developing countries, e.g., Philippines, Vietnam, Bangladesh. I want my relationships with my outsourcing workers to be mutually beneficial.

My outsourcing team really helps me with their creativity, energy, enthusiasm, skills in technology and desire to contribute. I am very grateful for their hard-work in developing my business and help in my own life personally. I really do view some of them as "my friends". I want their lives to be happy successful too.

I decided to proceed with outsourcing in my business, because I personally really enjoying interacting with people online (overseas), and the people I met through the outsourcing websites told me they want to work with me. Furthermore, outsourcing resources and techniques are effective and achieve productive results that I seek.

I don't fully understand how my outsourcing methods "fit in" into the big picture in the global economy. However, the way I see it is that the outsourcing workers I collaborated with over the last few years enjoy interactions with me and feel grateful for the income I provided them. I worked with some of my outsourcing teammates for over four years, and many for over a year.

I talked openly on video chat with my teammates about the ethical concerns that some GSP students introduced this year, and my outsourcing teammates feel we have a "win-win" relationship.

I would now like to highlight to you the benefits that outsourcing offers to providers:

Income

While a key benefit to consumers of outsourcing services is the associated lower cost, providers typically receive compensation that is competitive for providers' local market conditions; otherwise, the provider would reject the compensation being offered by the outsourcer and seek a different work opportunity. Hence, local market conditions typically (although, of course, not always) make outsourcing a "win-win" with respect to providers' compensation and consumers' costs.

Experience

Participating in outsourcing enables providers to practice and hone existing skills, and oftentimes acquire new ones. The providers' improved existing skills and newly acquired ones benefit both providers and consumers, since providers' enhanced skill sets make these providers' services more marketable, while those enhanced skills simultaneously benefit the consumer. Hence, "win-win".

Credentials

Closely related to the preceding point, providers' participation in an outsourced project enhances their credentials—it becomes an additional "arrow in their quiver" for trying to land additional and better work opportunities.

Networking

In my outsourcing, I have those working with me function as a team. This fosters creativity through different perspectives, divergent thinking, and brainstorming, as well as fostering synergy and a sense of community. We have frequent Internet-based team meetings, and each team member has every other provider's contact information. Each provider feels—and is—connected to, and supported by, the rest of the team. Team members use one another as information resources about project tasks, as well as about their own career development. This type of network-focused outsourcing fosters provider satisfaction and project productivity. Hence, "win-win".

Mentoring

Central to my approach to outsourcing is my role as a mentor. I am fortunate to have a strong educational background and extensive experience in Internet technology and entrepreneurship, as well as in team-based Internet project development. It is to my advantage to be the most effective mentor possible to the providers on my team—furthermore, my mentoring is a valuable educational benefit to the providers with whom I work. Hence, "win-win".

Making a Difference

The money we pay for goods and services is, of course, "a cost"—but it can also be an investment. Where and how we spend our own funds will, hopefully, have a beneficial impact on our success, but as entrepreneurs, we have to spend wisely with respect to our concerns about our "bottom line" and hopefully also with respect to our social consciences. Thoughtful use of outsourcing contributes to both of those goals. For example, rental housing in the Philippines averages one-seventh the cost in the US. Hence, if one takes a "global village" perspective on one's role as an entrepreneur, each dollar spent for services in the Philippines can have seven times the social impact of spending that same amount in the US—while also providing a substantially larger amount of services per dollar for your business. Hence, "win-win".

Introduction

Why Build Mobile App Software?

5.2 billion mobile phones are in use in the world as of 2014; this represents 73% of the world population[19]. 40% of these mobile phones are smartphones — 2.1 billion smartphones are already out there, including in the developing world. In 2014, 2.8 billion people were 'connected' to the Internet—while in 1995, just 80 million people had internet access. People are spending many hours a day—every day—with their smartphones. Building applications on top of the mobile platform has a potential to reach a wide range of people at an unprecedented growth rate—spreading like "wild fire" at a low-cost.

Steve Jobs, cofounder of Apple, holding up an iPhone smartphone.[20]

As you recall from Ray Kurzweil's presentations at Singularity University, the power of computing is advancing exponentially. The image

---

[19] Mary Meeker's "Internet Trends" presentation. http://www.kpcb.com/internet-trends

[20] https://remmeltmeijer.files.wordpress.com/2011/10/steve-jobs-holding-iphone.jpg

below depicting this trend originated from Ray Kurzweil's book, *The Singularity is Near.* [21] [22]

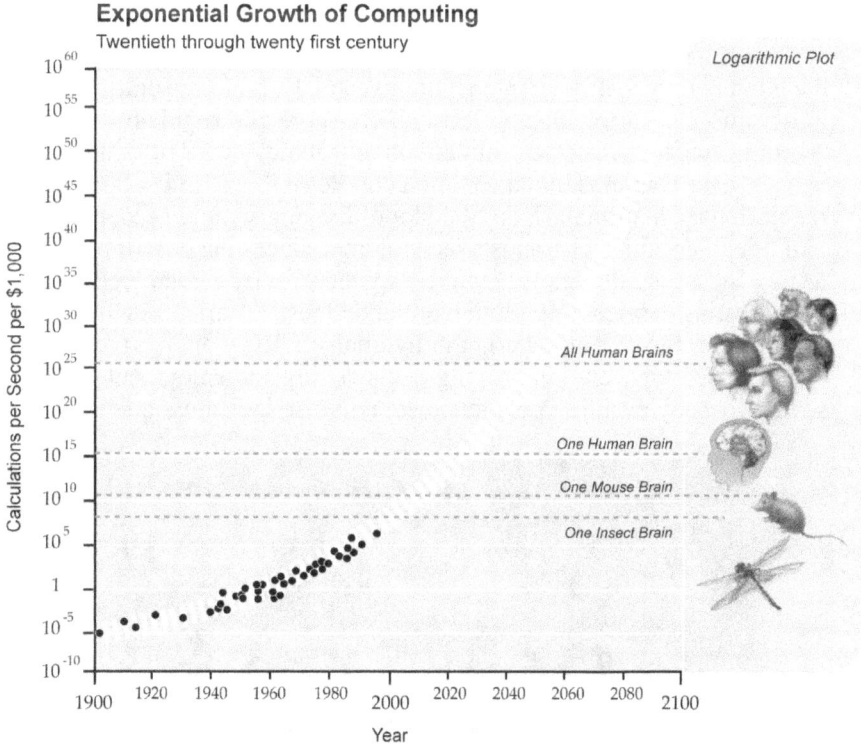

Smartphones are the most recent manifestation of exponentially improving technology. A computer as powerful as today's iPhone—in terms of computational speed—would occupy an entire building at MIT just 50 years ago, and this computer would cost $100+ million. Yet, now, this iPhone costs less than $1000. The modern smartphone fits in your pocket — "wired up" to a near ubiquitous wireless Internet and networking infrastructure—giving you access to information and knowledge resources greater than the President of the United States had available to him back in 1990.

---

[21] Kurzweil, R. (2005). The singularity is near: When humans transcend biology. Penguin.

[22] http://www.singularity.com/images/charts/ExponentialGrowthofComputing.jpg

These smartphone apps can affect people in "life-changing" ways. Smartphone applications can provide victims in a disaster with information about how to escape and help themselves evacuate to safety— this was a Singularity University (SU) team project from 2009, led by my classmate, Zubin Wadia. Mobile apps can enable family members to detect early indicators about a heart attack and save a loved one's life— a SU project.

Smartphone applications have the potential to change the world for the good and to positively impact the lives of 1+ billion people. Furthermore, smartphone applications can serve as a supplement to support "Grand Challenge" projects and effectively achieve your mission.

The Theranos blood testing technology [23] [24] —in itself—is revolutionary in miniaturizing the blood-drawing sample needed to test an individual's health. Theranos's technology reduces the cost of blood testing by practically one-seventh compared to current retail consumer blood testing services, e.g., Lab Corp and Quest. Theranos democratizes health information, empowering individuals to detect and correct serious health issues early on—improving one's quality and enjoyment of life, as saving lives by enabling people to catch disease indicators quicker.

Elizabeth Holmes, Founder of Theranos

---

[23] https://www.theranos.com

[24] Munro, D. (July 12, 2015). An Inside Look At The Theranos Direct-To-Consumer Experience. Forbes. From http://www.forbes.com/sites/danmunro/2015/07/13/an-inside-look-at-the-theranos-direct-to-consumer-experience/

To extend their impact further, the Theranos team produced an iPhone application [25] [26] that empowers individuals to receive their blood testing health results directly to their smartphones, even before their doctor! The Theranos iPhone application amplifies an individual's ability monitor health in real-time and take preventative action early—before irreversible symptoms become apparent and a life is taken "too soon". The Theranos iPhone application empowers individuals with data about their own body to make it actionable, not just some retrospective replay about your health a few weeks ago.

So, you might ask: Why build mobile applications software? The reason to build mobile application software is that this new platform suddenly makes accessible a vast range of extremely valuable—and even "life saving" information resources—that can both help the lives of people worldwide and benefit yourself as an entrepreneur in a successful business venture.

Instagram's Story of Exponential Growth

The story of Instagram's explosive exponential growth in users represents a good example of how fast a smartphone application can be distributed among millions of people. The Instagram application began—conceptually, in the mind of cofounders, Kevin Systrom and Mike Krieger[27]—as a "check-in" application—called 'Burbn." [28] This Burbn smartphone app concept had functionalities resembling Foursquare. However, after a few exposures to user feedback, the founders discovered

---

[25] https://itunes.apple.com/us/app/theranos/id915926715?mt=8

[26] http://1.bp.blogspot.com/-X4BRb8NEduA/VIuyH7EW_iI/AAAAAAAADYg/1SwkkPt2soo/s1600/holmes-1024x682.jpg

[27] https://www.flickr.com/photos/scobleizer/5222379928

[28] Markowitz, E. (April 10, 2012). How Instagram Grew From Foursquare Knock-Off to $1 Billion Photo Empire. From http://www.inc.com/eric-markowitz/life-and-times-of-instagram-the-complete-original-story.html

that the market didn't really seem to be very receptive to their product.

The Instagram founders changed directions towards focusing on just the photo-sharing component of the software they built. These entrepreneurs realized that they could create a compelling photo-sharing app by including the capabilities of (1) enabling users to add color filters to make their pictures look more attractive. In addition, they developed a technology to (2) allow photos to be uploaded "in the background" to the

cloud, to make publishing and sharing photos a faster and more seamless experience. Another notable design emphasis for Instagram included its functionality to (3) allow users to share photos rapidly with friends on social networks such as Facebook and Twitter.

Instagram went from zero users—just two guys experimenting with a mobile app concept—to 100 million users in just two years. [29] [30] The founders sold the company to Facebook for $1 billion within this two year period.[31]

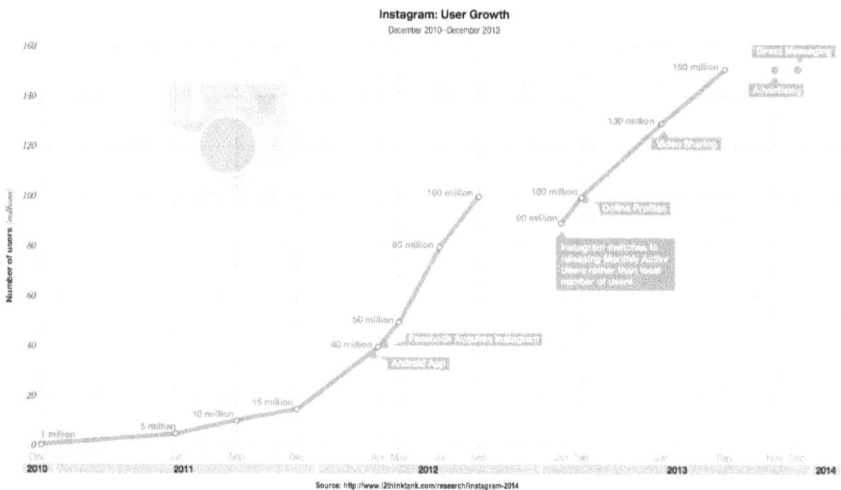

Instagram: User Growth
December 2010–December 2013

Source: http://www.l2thinktank.com/research/instagram-2014

---

[29] Spencer, G. (February 26, 2013). A Look Back At Instagram's Growth As It Hits 100 Million Monthly Active Users. From http://www.macstories.net/news/a-look-back-at-instagrams-growth-as-it-hits-100-million-monthly-active-users/

[30] http://heidicohen.com/wp-content/uploads/Instagram-User-Growth-Timeline-L2-Intelligence-Report2014.jpg

[31] Rusli, E. M. (2012). Facebook buys Instagram for $1 billion. New York Times.

The explosive growth and spread of Instagram on the mobile app platform give you a taste of what's possible when you build a really good app. You can reach hundreds of millions of people—perhaps even billions. You can have huge impact on the world and achieve dramatic business success.

The Instagram team size numbered less than 10 people when the app reached 10 million users. You don't even need a huge team and millions of dollars in investor funding to reach millions of users on the smartphone platform. You just need an idea, some mobile app developers, the courage to try it out in the market and get user feedback, and the patience, wherewithal, and creativity to reiterate your design and product until you achieve product-market fit.

If You Can't Code, Hire Coders.

Here's the problem: Many of you have amazing ideas. These ideas can solve the world's Grand Challenges. Singularity University admits an incredible class of brilliant students that really are empowered to change the world. However, not all of you have software development skills. Or, even if you can code, you need more programmers to make your dream a reality.

This book teaches you a solution: **Outsourcing**

With outsourcing, harness the talent of tens of thousands of programmers worldwide, especially in the Philippines, Bangladesh, China, Pakistan, India and Eastern Europe.

If you can't code, hire coders.

The below photo is of TJ, a computer programmer based in the Philippines, that I hired in early 2014. TJ, a recent university graduate, worked out of his parents' home in the Philippines, from his bunkbed in his bedroom. Just last July 2014, TJ's contributions to my business helped it to go, from languishing, to almost unimaginable personal success. I will help you find developers that will transform your business—and perhaps even your life and lifestyle.

Exoskeleton—Outsourcing Super Powers

When I think of outsourcing, I like to think of it as an exoskeleton —I am Ironman! The photo below shows a UC Berkeley research project where the person wearing an exoskeleton "strong man" suit ("Berkeley Lower Extremity Exoskeleton") has enhanced leg muscle strength to carry heavy objects. [32]   With my outsourcing, I gain almost "superhuman" powers. Superpowers! I acquire these powers through outsourcing and hiring people overseas to do my work.

When you outsource, you are still the center of the business and team. Your skills are the origin source of capabilities. Achievements center on your own skills, thoughts, desires and goals. Your desires are control the direction of the business. Your thoughts are the dominant thinking of the team. Your goals have the highest priority.

---

[32] http://bleex.me.berkeley.edu/wp-content/uploads/hel-media/images/CV/ Berkeley-Exo-HR.jpg http://bleex.me.berkeley.edu

Your "muscles" are the center of everything. Yet, your muscles amplified through the outsourcing. Thus, outsourcing feels like you're wearing an exoskeleton. You are Iron Man. You can lift objects that are heavier than you could have otherwise. You can jump higher. You can run faster. Overall, you are more powerful. With outsourcing, you have superpowers to achieve your vision and imagination like never before.

Take Baby Steps—A Cautionary Tale

I gave a talk on outsourcing at Draper University in San Mateo, CA, back in 2013, and I was also a student there too. Draper University—founded by venture capitalist, Tim Draper—is a school for "Super Heroes", entrepreneurs with "Super Powers". This school also calls upon its alumni to "change the world" and help others through technology innovation and entrepreneurship success.

I had a classmate at Draper University—I'll call her "Sarah" in this book to protect her identity. Sarah got really excited about her website idea. Sarah wanted to build a global university online where professors could upload lecture videos and educate the world through their teachings.

Sarah went on UpWork.com (called oDesk.com at the time), and she found a developer in Russia that claimed he could build exactly what she envisioned: website to serve as a global video university. The Russian developer told Sarah, "I can build exactly what you want for $35,000. And, all you need to do is just pay me half of the money up front."

Within the first three or four days of experimenting with her new outsourcing techniques, Sarah wire transferred $17,500 to this Russian developer. And—as you can imagine—of course, after a month, Sarah still did not have the website that she really wanted and envisioned. The developer didn't want to give the money back, because he felt he had put it in his own valuable time and energy into the project. Thus, Sarah basically wasted $17,500. Not only that, this wasted money represented almost one-third of her own personal savings that she could have directed into furthering her graduate education.

Don't do what Sarah did. Do not take Sarah's path. Don't go spent a lot of money early on. You need to take baby steps. Early on, give out little tasks for $5. Get comfortable communicating with remote workers. Don't expect a lot to be accomplished in the beginning. Expect little small tasks to be accomplished rapidly for a small cost. Once you're comfortable with this level of efficiency and time savings, build up to $100 tasks. Definitely do not wire transfer $10,000. And, certainly do not wire transfer $17,500 in the first three or four days using outsourcing techniques—even if the developer appears really nice and confident.

Funnel Hiring

How Funnel Hiring Works

Through my experience outsourcing, I discovered that a good way to think about finding developers and staff members is as a funnel. [33] This hiring funnel works like this:

- You need to start with considering a broad range of potential candidates for your job.
- You need to somehow get the attention of available candidates — either by posting a job on one of the outsourcing websites, or by sending out direct invitations or emails to candidates with published work profiles or resumes.
- Among the candidates that express interest in your job, you need to test these individuals through a series of "Performance Tests".
- Finally, after a series of tests, you incorporate the discovered individual into your team — hiring him or her and working closely through various communication and collaboration tools available online.

Outsourcing Hiring Process

- Select and visit outsourcing website
- Register as employer
- Browse and search worker profiles
- Post a job
- Send invitations to your job
- Reply to messages from candidates
- Arrange Skype video chat meetings and interviews
- Make hiring offers

The Funnel Hiring process is made up of three primary components: **People**, **Performance Tests**, and **Communication and Collaboration**.

The supply of **People** available on the outsourcing networks, such as UpWork.com or OnlineJobs.ph is your 'starting point' of available candidates.

Performance Tests help you to identify the 'best of the best' developers, and filter out individuals that don't have the required technical skills. Your tests also filter out developers that do not have sufficient time availability or interest in your job.

---

[33] Toterhi, T., & Recardo, R. J. (2013). The Talent Funnel: How to Surface Key Human Resources. Global Business and Organizational Excellence, 32(5), 22-44.

After you conduct a series of Performance Tests, you are left with 'genius' developers. These genius developers have the skills needed to build your app; they are motivated and actually available for your job. The testing process helps you avoid wasting time and money on people that won't really "deliver the goods" for you in the end.

At the end of your tests, 'genius' developers remain, and you move into the **Communication and Collaboration** phase. You communicate and collaborate with your discovered genius—using the best available online tools, whatever they may be at this point in time, e.g., Skype video chat, GoToMeeting, Slack, Asana. Communication tools are constantly changing online, and you would be wise to use whatever are the best available tools and resources to give your team the strongest competitive advantage.

Funnel Hiring

- People Supply
- Performance Tests
- Communication & Collaboration

Integrate this genius into your team and, basically, "make friends". Perhaps, you video chat together on Skype everyday—ensuring that the app you want gets built and the product gets modified rapidly based on feedback from users. Make corrections based on your own intuitions about the functionality and design of the app.

To "flesh out" this "Hiring Funnel" metaphor, consider the image below. The *liquid* represents the potential outsources workers you might hire — the "People". The *funnel* is the series of "Performance Tests" that the candidates must undergo for you to consider them for the position. At each stage of testing, the potential candidates become smaller and smaller — either because the candidates do not have necessary skills or because the candidates lose interest in your hiring process. A more narrow *straw* at the bottom is left for the 'genius' developers that you discovered through your recruitment and testing process. Now that you identified these geniuses, you *consume* them into your team. The geniuses, ideally, integrate into your team and propel your business forward through their talents and contributions.

The analogy of a funnel applies to understand effective recruiting, testing and selection of outsourcing developers online.

Perhaps this metaphor of the funnel is not quite accurate, because what you're doing is actually "filtering out" or excluding potential candidates. In other words, you are discarding individuals that do not pass your performance tests. Whereas, in the funnel metaphor, represented in the photo, in fact, all the liquid passes through the funnel and through the straw at the bottom. All of the liquid would actually be consumed — none of it discarded—if the funnel is held upright long enough. Nevertheless, I think this funnel metaphor is a good "visual" to help you remember to consider a "wide range" of potential candidates—and, also that, an effective entrepreneur is wise to test developer candidates repeatedly, in order to discover the 'best of the best' available people to build mobile apps.

Recruiting Your Developers

Let's get even more concrete in our discussion about recruiting your outsourcing workers. Suppose you want to hire a developer or a set of developers to help you build an iPhone application. An effective approach is to break down the app you envision into a couple functional components.

For example, perhaps you want to build a photo-sharing mobile application. Suppose your app needs to be able to (1) capture a photo, (2) allow the user to input some text, (3) store the data up on the cloud, such as through parse.com, and (4) display helpful information.

In this scenario, you would want to test that the candidate mobile app developers could successfully perform each of the four component functionalities described above. The details of the app are not important at this point, e.g., a photo-sharing app targeted to young moms that want to share cooking recipes with their friends. You just need to test the developers' capabilities to build the component functionalities. And, the more developers that you can find that possess such capabilities, the better off you are! You'll be able to be even more selective about other attributes of your workers once you established the set of individuals that have the necessary technology skills. You'll be able to next select for workers that have actual time availability to work with you, or that can be available on a timezone that you're awake — or the cheapest bidder.

In this situation, I would make the initial performance test very simple — the equivalent of a "Hello World" iPhone application. In such a "Hello World" application, the developer might just simply need to build a working app that prints "Hello World" on the screen and displays a photo. That's a beginning to give you verification that the developer would be able to achieve building capability (4) above.

Funnel Hiring: An Example In Action

- Hire 100 Developers on Same Small Relevant Coding Task
- Performance Tests (Wufoo.com)
- Discover "Geniuses"
- Make Friends with Geniuses!

Also, you will be amazed that this first simple test will likely filter out a significant chunk of the 'active candidates' in the pool of individuals you're considering for the job. For example, oftentimes, 'firms' of developers don't want to deal with such simple programming tests. In these 'firms', there are often 'business negotiators' in the front-lines communicating with you. These business guys are not personally able to build even such a simple "Hello World" app. So, your Performance Test might exclude out developer teams like this. That's usually a good thing, in my experience, because the business guys often make the price of the project expensive for you, and they don't "deliver the goods" as well as working directly with a genius computer programmer that you can video chat with and give rapid feedback to in the iterations of your application development.

When you hire single individual geniuses— especially Full-Time Filipinos—you can seamlessly integrate them into your team, your workflow and your life! "Firm" developer groups—particularly in India and Pakistan—will likely be more mercenary, more expensive, less productive, less loyal and less fun to work with.

Once this initial simple "Hello World" application has been built by your currently active job candidates, then you give another test. For example, next, you might test on application functionality (1) capture a photo. You might ask the developers to build an app to capture a photo, save it to the file system and then present it back to the user in some interface. A good developer should be able to build these Performance Test apps in 45 minutes—"pocket change" in a competent developer's time. Notice that the app functionality is tested piece-by-piece — not "all at once" in some big project that might take days to build. Again, this test will filter out the candidates.

Next, among the candidates that remain, design a performance test centered on demonstrating app functionality (2), allow the user to input some text. Create a mockup and instructions detailing exactly how this simple functionality should work. Give this instruction to the available developer candidates. Collect their code submissions and, again, evaluate the submissions as Pass or Fail. Discard those that Fail. And, continue the testing process on the developers that Pass.

Next, test for functionality (3), store data up on the cloud. Design a test that would require the user captured data to be stored up on the cloud — whether text data or photo files. It doesn't need to be the functionality precisely as you envision it for your "end product" app. It's just functionality demonstrating that this particular developer 'could' build what you would like in the end.

And, again, this performance test that you design is simple. You don't want the performance test to be too complex or time consuming for the candidates — because, otherwise, you will get steeper attrition in the active candidates than desired. If your test is too difficult or time consuming, you will filter out candidates that have the skills that you desire; they may not want to "put up with" the hassle of the tests that you're presenting to them. These candidates might also fear that they will spend a lot time on your project — and, yet, in the end, you might never pay them or hire them for the "real" project.

At this point, after four tests, it's likely that you have filtered down your list of active candidates to more than 50%. Perhaps even only 20% or 10% of the original candidates made it this far. If your percentage is lower than 10%, consider revising your testing process to make your tests "easier" and "faster" to build — and, then start your recruitment and hiring process over again from the starting point. Remember that you're testing for basic coding abilities — not asking the developers to build the "real thing" at this point. Try to shoot for a good developer being able to complete each of your tests in 45 minutes.

Also, to incentivize candidates, you might consider paying the candidates for successful completion of each of the performance tests. For example, you might pay candidates $1 for completion of test #1 via PayPal. Then you might pay $2 for completion of test #2. $4 for test #3. $8 for test #4. Then you won't feel you're wasting the time of the candidates, and the candidates will know that you're very serious about this recruitment process, and they have a real chance at 'winning the prize' of joining your team and having a job working with you longterm.

As you can imagine, if you're dealing with hundreds or even thousands of interested developers for your job, it would be overly time consuming to collect the candidates' submissions for their performance tests via email or Skype chat. To scale up, you need to use a web form such as wufoo.com or google doc forms. An advantage of using these forms is that you can make information 'required' for submission. For example, you might make the candidates' emails required. Candidates' emails are helpful to collect because you can 'email blast' everyone at once with instructions about your recruitment process, e.g., point candidates to the next test in your testing process.

Also, getting candidates' Skype usernames is helpful. If you have developers' Skype, you can add them as contacts and jump straight into a video chat interview. I've personally done that a number of times. Sometimes, I will review candidates' code submissions and feel so impressed that I want to immediately video chat and make a hiring offer. With the top developers, they can get "scooped up" fast, and sometimes, you really need jump to take him or her off the job market.

The following is a list of candidate information that I like to collect as part of the recruitment process:
- **Name**
- **Email**
- **Skype username**
- **Work Profile URL Link**, e.g., UpWork.com, OnlineJobs.ph

It's helpful to make each of the above data fields required. You might want to include an example of what an accurate 'Work Profile URL Link' looks like, because without that example, I see many candidates input an incorrect URL link.

At times, I might include additional fields to a candidate's form submission for a Performance Test:

- **Bitbucket.org or Github.com username** — Perhaps I might want to share a code repository with a candidate as a "starting project" code base for the test. Or, perhaps, I'll ask for test submissions to be made through such a code repository. Another advantage of retrieving a candidates' username for such a code repository website is that you can visit the repositories the candidate previously uploaded or worked with and evaluate the strength of his or her programming skills through prior work.

Submission Field And, finally, you would want to have some field for the candidates' Performance Test submissions. This submission might simply be a text area field, where a candidate might paste in the text code of her answer. Or, the submission field might be a file upload, where a completed iPhone project might be 'zipped' together in a compressed file and uploaded to a server for your later download and review.

Alternatively, the submission might take the form of a youtube.com or vimeo.com video URL link. In this video, the developer demonstrates the app working via a screen recording video.

The submission field might take on any form you can imagine. Remember, though, that you want to keep your performance tests simple and fast for competent developers to complete; otherwise, your candidate attrition will be too high, and you will exclude perfectly capable and productive potential workers — and deprive yourself from the benefits of those workers' contributions to your team.

I will next describe more in detail the core components of the Funnel Hiring process: People, Performance Tests, and Communication and Collaboration.

People Supply

Where Do I Like to Find My Workers?

In order to successfully outsource, you need a supply of people. Outsourcing is performed by people. To be effective at getting your projects built, you need effective and talented people — as well as, people with time availability, and, of course, affordable people. The best way to find people with the 'optimal' attributes described above is to consider a vast range of available workers and to test them through Performance Tests. These tests ensure they "have what it takes". But, how do you find this 'starting point' set of available workers? You find them online, of course. But, where? My favorite places now are: OnlineJobs.ph and UpWork.com

OnlineJobs.ph
UpWork.com

A number of websites are available online with webpages representing available workers. I call these resources: "Outsourcing Websites". At the time of this writing, UpWork.com is the largest such "Outsourcing Website" to my knowledge. Other such large outsourcing websites include Elance.com and freelancer.com.

You can visit these outsourcing websites and see lists of available workers. You can register for a free account on the Outsourcing websites and become an active 'employer' to give you the authority to contact workers with job invitations and hire them into your team for work. Oftentimes, a "worker profile" page represents each available worker. These profile pages are similar to Facebook or LinkedIn profile pages. A list of skills or experience with programming languages is outlined on these worker profile pages. In the case of UpWork.com, you can see the "work history" of actual verified prior projects that the worker accomplished, including the dollar amount paid and number of hours worked.

I would like to describe my two current favorite Outsourcing Websites in more detail: OnlineJobs.ph and UpWork.com.

I usually look to OnlineJobs.ph first when I do recruiting, because the site contains a repository of resumes from solely Filipinos. I discovered, over the past two years, that Filipinos are particularly great and effective, in general, at helping me with my online business — compared to outsource workers from other countries. I will describe later in this book the reasons for this preference.

Additionally, I like to recruit workers from UpWork.com, especially when I need to find mobile app developers and people with significantly advanced technical skills. Sometimes, I find that OnlineJobs.ph (Filipino workers) just simply doesn't have enough available computer programmers, particularly in the mobile app domain. So, I've got to "cast my net out" more broadly when I search for mobile app developers.

Certainly, other outsourcing websites exist. And, I'm sure I could find some great workers there too. However, usually, it just isn't necessary for me to conduct my recruiting search beyond OnlineJobs.ph and UpWork.com. For your benefit, however, I will list some of these other outsourcing websites next that you can check out.

Broader Networks of Available Outsourcing Workers

The following contains a list of some of the top outsourcing websites. I know you can find an even bigger list of outsourcing sites by just googling the topic. However, this list will provide you a good launching point with literally millions of online workers available for you to hire. Some of the sites are a better fit for finding mobile app developers such as UpWork.com, Elance.com, and GetACoder.com. Other sites on the list are awesome at finding "back office" type workers — e.g., data entry, customer service—such as OnlineJobs.ph or PeoplePerHour.

Amazon Mechanical Turk is a bit of a different model — you hire workers for specific limited tasks ("Human Intelligence Tasks"). On Amazon Mechanical Turk, you will likely never actually "meet" the workers on Skype video chat—though, I suppose it's possible. Instead of hiring individuals for a long term working relationship and video chatting with them, the work tasks are likely 'transactional' and not involving in depth collaboration and rapport building among a team of colleagues. Amazon Mechanical Turk is really effective for hiring hundreds of people for some small, limited, low-cost task, e.g., data entry, audio transcription or pattern recognition.

People Supply

Full-Time Filipinos:

OnlineJobs.ph
BestJobs.ph

More Outsourcing Sites:

UpWork.com	Craigslist.com	99designs
Elance.com	GetACoder	Amazon Mechanical Turk
Guru.com	iFreelance	PeoplePerHour
Freelancer.com	SimplyHired	Twago.com

99designs is also a bit different in that it's focused on graphical design — mobile app screens, icons, design of logos, webpages, marketing material. You post a project with a description of what's needed; you get designers to bit for your project and submit proposals; you give feedback for iterations on the design; then finally, you pay the "winner" designer. 99designs is great for generating artwork and icons for your mobile app. However, you will likely not integrate these designers into your team as seamlessly as Full-Time Filipinos.

Full-Time Filipinos

I'd like to introduce you to some members of my team: Full-time outsourcing workers based in the Philippines. You can see some of their photos below. First, I would like to say that the English skills of Filipinos are excellent. [34] I have many more positive things to say about people from the Philippines, especially their kind interactions with me and affinity

---

[34] Friginal, E. (2007). Outsourced call centers and English in the Philippines. World Englishes, 26(3), 331-345.

for Western culture. [35] I'll first describe to you my early learning experiences associated with outsourcing.

When I first started my learning curve of outsourcing, I began by hiring people on outsourcing websites without considering their country of origin. The workers I hired came from India, Pakistan, Bangladesh, Eastern Europe and South America and all throughout Asia. I even hired some Americans early on to help me figure out some details with dedicated server setup. I quickly learned that hiring Americans—as well as Europeans—were way too expensive and not even close to my range of "affordability".

I learned to focus on hiring people in the developing world, because they were far more affordable and their work quality was usually sufficient, and sometimes even excellent. Furthermore, even their English

abilities (both writing and verbal skills) can be superb—more than adequate to communicate with me online and get work done.

As I gained experience outsourcing, I discovered a set of lecture videos produced by a successful outsourcing entrepreneur, employer and teacher, named John Jonas. http://www.jonasblog.com John Jonas help me to discover a third transformative technique for outsourcing. That transformative technique for me is: Hire exclusively Full-Time Filipinos.

Through John Jonas's teachings, I discovered that Filipinos are an exceptionally productive source of workers for your online business. Their English is great. They understood what you said. They don't pretend like

---

[35] Leavitt, N. (2007). The changing world of outsourcing. Computer, 40(12), 13-16.

they understood—nodding her head—and yet, they really had no clue. They will communicate with you directly about ideas. They will even disagree with you vigorously. They personally want to be successful, and they want you to be successful. Many of your Full-Time Filipinos will genuinely care about you and the success of the team. They care about you as the owner of the business and want the business to succeed. They are loyal. They will even become your friends. And, some know how to computer program.

Many other entrepreneurs and businesses learned that the Philippines is a particularly helpful place to look in recruiting your team of outsourcing workers. [36] [37] [38] [39]

Your team of Full-Time Filipinos will become your "superpower" exoskeleton that I described earlier in this book.

Five hours of John Jonas' trainings videos about hiring Full-Time Filipinos are available on his Udemy.com course at: https://www.udemy.com/how-to-hire-talented-virtual-assistants-from-the-philippines/

You can also visit John Jonas' blog for more tips: http://www.jonasblog.com/philippines-outsourcing-tip-1-of-16-daily-communication

I learned from John Jonas the very important concept of hiring your workers as "exclusive" Full-Time—using the "One Job Policy" in hiring and managing your Filipino team. By saying, Full-Time, I mean that your workers work for you 40 hours per week, and your job is their only exclusive job. The worker isn't allowed to "moonlight" or take on other "clients" or income streams. This is your "One Job Policy" as an employer. As John Jonas spoke about in his blog and teaching videos, you get a four times increase productivity when your outsourced workers have only one job—working for you. Because, if your workers have other jobs and other income sources, then your success and the success of your online business don't really matter.

_____

[36] Olchondra, R. T. (2006). As India gets too costly, BPOs turn to Philippines. The Philippine Daily Inquirer.

[37] Munoz, J. M., & Welsh, D. H. (2006). Outsourcing in the IT industry: the case of the Philippines. The International Entrepreneurship and Management Journal, 2(1), 111-123.

[38] Lockwood, J. (2010). Consulting assessment for the business processing outsourcing (BPO) industry in the Philippines. Globalization, communication and the workplace, 221-41.

[39] Sahay, S., Nicholson, B., & Krishna, S. (2003). Global IT outsourcing. Software Development across borders, 1.

The techniques of hiring Full-Time Filipinos that I described above is a unique form of outsourcing. In the past, when people would think about outsourcing, they would think about hiring computer programmers in India. That is not the optimal approach in my experience.

Furthermore, a separate and different approach to outsourcing is hiring freelancers—people working online from outsourcing websites such as Elance.com, oDesk.com, and UpWork.com. Certainly, you can get a lot of work done with these freelancers. These freelancers have skills and programming capabilities that you did not, and they will gladly contribute to your business in ways that can blow your mind.

However, compared to Full-Time long-term Filipino employees, Freelancers have major shortcomings. Freelancers from those type of outsourcing websites often have multiple clients, multiple different projects, and multiple different income streams. Their loyalty is very much divided. They are hopping from one contract to the next.

As an employer and owner, you cannot step away from the business and expect freelancers to continue their work. With freelancers, you must be constantly supervising and directing their work.

In contrast, with Full-Time Filipinos, you can step away from the business—perhaps going to vacation to Europe—and your outsourced workers will continue to operate the business. They will look after your customers and sales processes, and keep your business afloat. I found that keeping my team populated with almost all Full-Time Filipinos has been a "secret sauce" to my business's success in the past year.

Worker Profiles On Outsourcing Websites

I would like to now described to you in more detail about how you can find, recruit, and collaborate with outsourced online workers. I give special emphasis to methods associated with finding Full-Time Filipinos, because that is my favorite approach in my outsourcing techniques that I currently utilize.

Outsourcing Hiring Process

- Select and visit outsourcing website
- Register as employer
- Browse and search worker profiles
- Post a job
- Send invitations to your job
- Reply to messages from candidates
- Arrange Skype video chat meetings and interviews
- Make hiring offers

First, you need to know about the best available outsourcing websites—the websites that have the most online workers. You need to know about the outsourcing websites with the best workers: the highest skilled and most effective workers. In the preceding section, I already described examples of such outsourcing websites. At the time that you read this, other—perhaps better—websites might exist. I'm sure you can find these by simply googling "outsourcing websites". Currently, as I said, my favorite websites for recruiting my workers are OnlineJobs.ph and UpWork.com. UpWork.com is were I would focus my attention on most if I was searching for a mobile app developer.

Once you select your outsourcing websites for recruitment, you need to visit the websites and sign up as an employer. On UpWork.com, you can make an account as an employer for free. On OnlineJobs.ph, you need to pay for an employer account, and that's $50 per month.

The advantage of OnlineJobs.ph, though, is that once you pay for your employer account, you have no more fees to pay the site. In contrast, with UpWork.com, you are expected to pay your workers through the outsourcing site itself, and UpWork.com takes roughly a 10% additional transaction fee over your contractors' earnings. When you register for an account, you simply provide your name, your email and your payment information, such as a credit card or PayPal account details.

As a registered employer, you have access to contact prospective employees. Basically, now, you can send job candidates emails and messages inviting them to your job. You can also browse worker profiles and do searches for skills, in order to find the workers that will best fit your needs. On most outsourcing websites, you can, in fact, browse worker profiles even before you register as an employer.

Once you are ready to invite job candidates to your position, you can post a job on the outsourcing network website. You will receive applications from candidates through the website's messaging system inbox and emails. Also, you can create a list of candidates that you found through searching and browsing, and you can send candidates an invitation to your job with a targeted and direct message.

When you reach out to candidates and receive applications, you can have conversations with those candidates through email and through the website's messaging system. Additionally, you can communicate—and collect contact information and testing submissions—through web forms ("Performance Tests") that I will describe in more detail later in this book. Consider inviting candidates to video chat or voice only interviews on Skype or GoToMeeting. The type of testing, interviews and selection you do depends on your own preferences, time constraints and cost considerations.

At this point, after you've performed a few tests and interviews, now is the time to hire one or more people. As I will describe later in this book, I like to hire a bunch of people for a position. Only after working with people for a while do you discover if they really have the skills and time needed to assist you in your business. By hiring a bunch of people, you can be more confident that—a few weeks down the road—you have at least one person that has the skills, desires and time to really contribute to your business. This is the "Funnel Hiring" process that I will describe in more depth later. "Funnel Hiring" is a process of starting with a large volume of candidates under consideration for a job, and "narrowing down" these candidates based on tests and requests to produce actual work that closely approximates the results that you seek. The filtering process of candidates is like taking the candidates out for a "test drive" in a car you might buy.

Let's take a look at some specific outsourcing websites and do some searches—so, you get the idea of how to find candidates for your job. We will focus our search on finding mobile app developers; although, this methodology can be applied to finding workers for a broad range of skill sets needed for your business, e.g., sales and data entry.

The image below shows a screenshot of OnlineJobs.ph after we perform a search for "android developers". We can see that 208 android developers are available. The search results show specific people available for work, including the developers' photos, the number of hours in a week people are available, desired salary per month, and prior work experiences. Furthermore, we see a score on "Identification proof", representing some background information collected by the outsourcing website on the validity of the person's identity. Some of these identity verifications include government IDs, birth certificates, and university records. We also

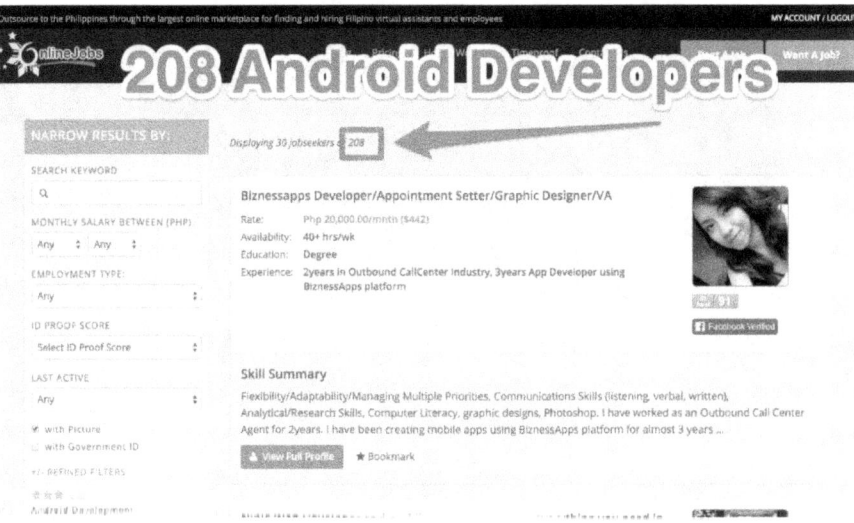

see if the user is "Facebook verified", which is another method to validate a person's profile.

The panel at the left side allows the employer to filter through candidates further—to narrow down to the "right one". This type of more detailed filtering includes searching based on desired salary per month in pesos—which is the currency of the Philippines. Also, you can search for people available Full-Time or Part-Time. You can filter based on the ID score, as well as whether or not the job candidates provided the outsourcing website a validated government identification card. You can search by specific self-reported scores on skills, such as android development skills, or perhaps iPhone development skills. You can search based on self-reported capabilities in the English language—English verbal or writing capabilities. All of these skills are self-reported; so, you have the responsibility as an employer to perform confirmation skill tests in order to ensure that individuals have the capabilities to contribute to your business as expected.

Consider now at a specific worker profile on OnlineJobs.ph. The below mobile app developer desires a rate of 20,000 pesos per month, which translates to $442 per month. Furthermore, at this rate, this mobile app developer is available to you Full-Time, 40 hours per week. We see that he has seven years of experience in graphic design and three years of experience in mobile and web development. He appears to be a college student perhaps, or maybe a college graduate. In fact, he is already employed by one employer. So, if you want to have the Full-Time exclusive "One Job Policy" in place, you might want to be looking at other candidates instead. It looks like he is "Facebook verified", and a more

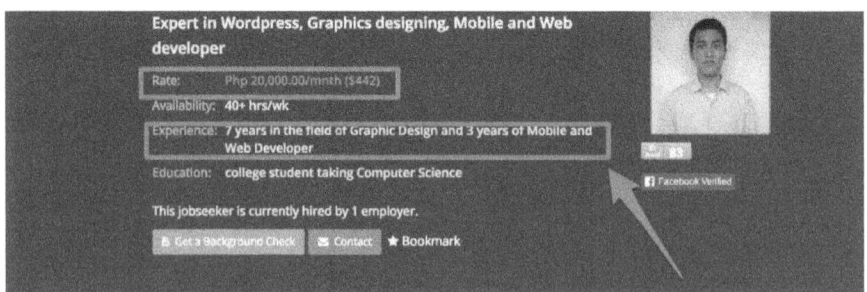

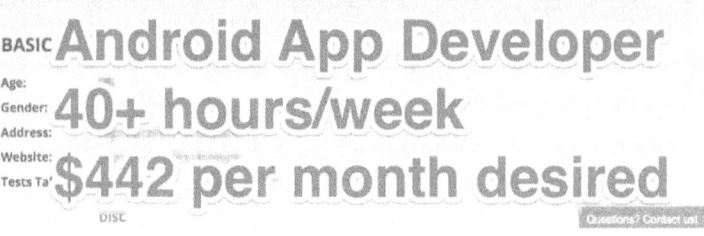

extensive background check is available. You are free to contact him by simply clicking the "contact" button. This contact button will allow you to send a message and email to the candidate. Then, the candidate has a choice on whether to reply and respond to your invitation, in order to progress forward in the hiring process.

Oftentimes, I see responses to my job invitations within hours, and even within minutes. Unemployment in the Philippines is high. Online jobs—where people can work at their houses out of their bedrooms—are coveted. Online jobs can frequently have numerous advantages compared to local physical jobs: a relatively large salary, the flexibility from working at home surrounded by family, and a lack of transportation and food costs associated with a commune to work in the city.

In the below worker profile, we see that the developer claims to have iOS and iPhone programming skills. He is also looking to make 20,000 pesos per month, which corresponds to $442 per month. He claims to have skills in word press development, PHP programming, C# and .Net programming, as well as, iOS and iPhone programming. He states that he

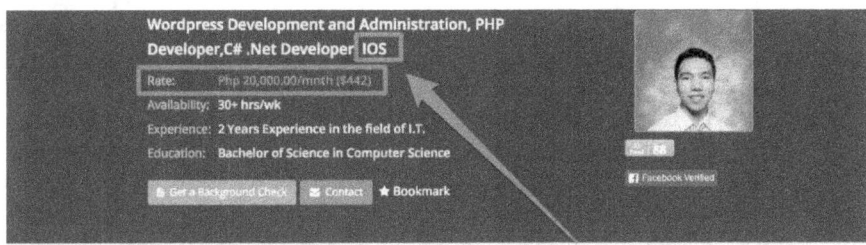

has a Bachelors of Science degree in Computer Science. Also, he says that he has two years of experience in Information Technology. You are also free to contact this candidate by simply clicking the "contact" button. You can send him a message and email him in this way to proceed forward in the hiring process—and to perhaps integrate him into your team and build a mobile application together.

Consider performing a search for iOS developers on OnlineJobs.ph. 133 iOS developers are available through this outsourcing website. The first candidate is looking for 50,000 pesos per month

($1,106) for Full-Time work. He has a bachelors degree and five years of experience as a developer and designer. We can look more in depth at search results to find additional candidates.

Next, let's do a search for PHP developers. You might want to hire a PHP developer to build a server–side component for your mobile app business. For example, you might want to push data—such as text and photos—to the cloud and make it available to your mobile app users. We see a search on OnlineJobs.ph yields 3,796 PHP developers. Again, we can filter using the panel on the left based on skills, keywords, the desired

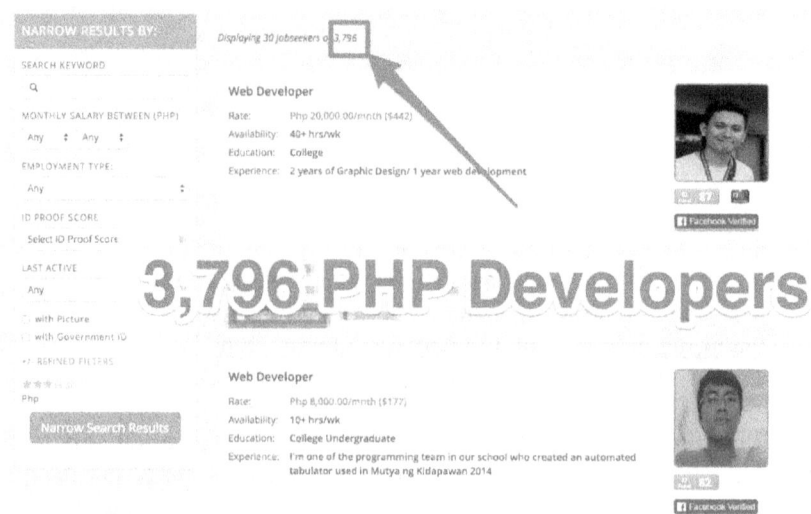

monthly salary, employment type, ID proof, when the candidate was last active on the website and Government ID. In our search results, we see a preview of the available candidates, and you can review the details of the candidates' profiles, where you can invite them to your job.

Let's consider some other outsourcing websites. Below, we have a screenshot of Elance.com. Elance has hundreds of thousands of profiles of freelancers. You can see that there are 6,218 mobile app developers that appear on the search results. Again, you can use the left panel to filter candidates down further based on more detailed criteria.

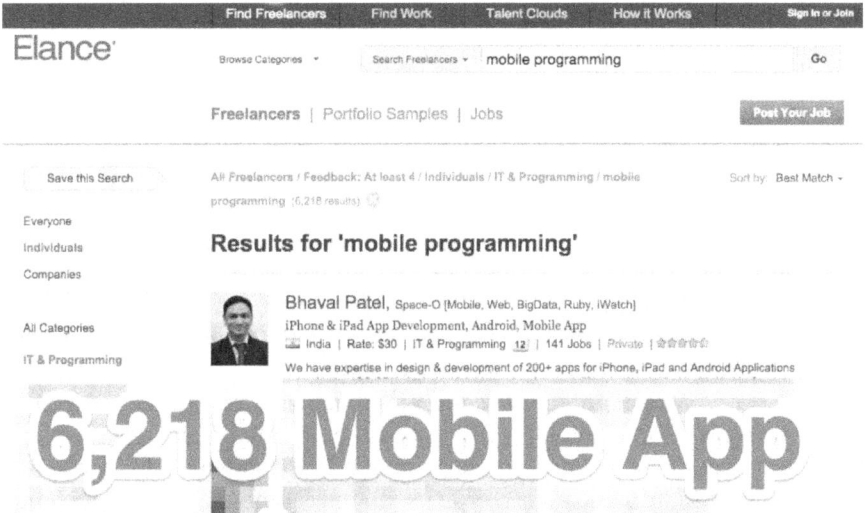

Let's look now at the enormous network, UpWork.com. A search for mobile app developers on UpWork.com yields 96,820 people. That's huge! Surely you will be able to find someone that can help you with your project with such a large quantity of mobile app developers available to

you online. You are free to discover your own preferences and techniques to test candidates and then to collaborate with your worker together to get your applications built.

Getting Candidate Workers: Sending Invitations and Posting Jobs

I will describe in more detail about how to get the attention of outsourcing workers and candidates for your jobs, enabling you to advance candidates through your recruitment and testing process.

The screen below shows the 'send a message' page on OnlineJobs.ph. This is the page you see after you press the "contact" button on candidates' work profiles. You see the name of the candidate that you are about to send a message—as well as some of his or her qualifications. You have a place to put your name. You have a place to put your own email. You have a box to input the subject line of your message. And, finally, you have the message itself that you will be sending to candidates to invite them to your job. Furthermore, to make things easier for you, the website provides an ability to save a template message, which is a previous message sent to candidates with the information needed to continue on in your recruitment process.

Writing effective recruitment messages can be an 'art form'. However, for a beginner, you can simply say that you have a job and that you want the candidate to meet you on Skype video chat for an interview. Of course, provide your Skype username. A more advanced technique is to send a link in your invitation message to a web form such as Wufoo.com or

Google docs, where candidates will provide contact information and begin your skill testing process—a technique that I call "Performance Tests".

The screen below shows how to post a job on UpWork.com. You simply write the job title. You specify which "Team" the job is associated with. You classify the job in a category. In this case, the job is in the "web, mobile and software development" category—specifically, mobile development. You also write a detailed text description of the job in the large box. You can also upload some diagrams, images, sketches or PDFs that outline the details of the project further.

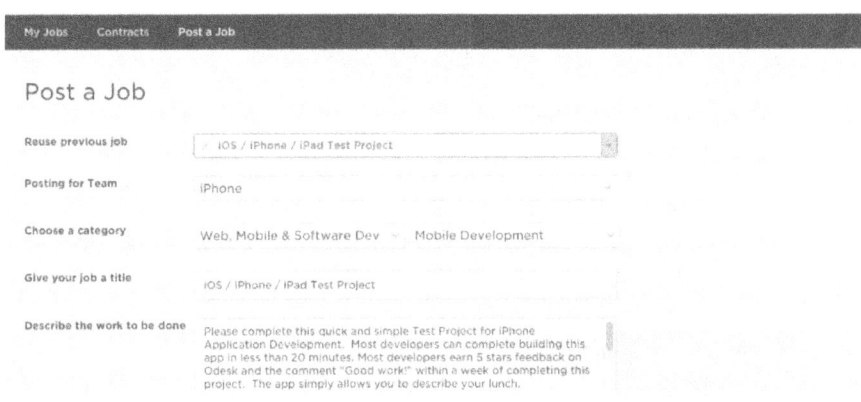

Employment Contracts on UpWork.com

Outsourcing websites differ in how they handle hiring and employment. In the case of OnlineJobs.ph, the website simply serves as a repository of resumes, where you can browse and contact candidates through the site by sending a message or email. From there, you to hire and pay your workers directly, such as through PayPal or Xoom. You might write your own employment contracts—or, maybe even never bother with it at all.

In contrast, other outsourcing websites require you to hire your workers through the website with an official "employment contract", enforced and mediated by the site itself; you are expected to pay your workers through the website. On some of these sites, paying your workers directly and not mediated through the outsourcing website is viewed as a violation of the terms of service. If you are found violating the terms of service (known as "working outside of UpWork"), you can be banned permanently. These types of outsourcing websites oftentimes take a percentage of the money paid to your outsourcing workers, such as 10% fee on top of their salary. The advantage to you as an employer is that the outsourcing website can sometimes help you "get your money back" if somehow you feel you have not gotten the results that you have expected. Furthermore, the outsourcing websites can hold your money in escrow. In these cases, the workers might feel more confident with the money being held by the outsourcing website; this reduces the risk to the workers that he or she will not get paid for work accomplished.

You can see below the worker profile of Asmi S., located in Rawalpinidi, Pakistan—whom I hired a few years ago. She actually did not help me computer program. She assisted me more with business processes, including data entry, development of business strategy, and making sales telephone calls. On her profile, you can see that she requests a rate of $6.67 per hour. Also, you can see some of her skills, her work history and experience. In fact, she worked over 15,000 hours on the UpWork.com outsourcing platform. Her work hours were verified using the proprietary UpWork.com time tracking software, which include screenshots and keyboard click monitoring.

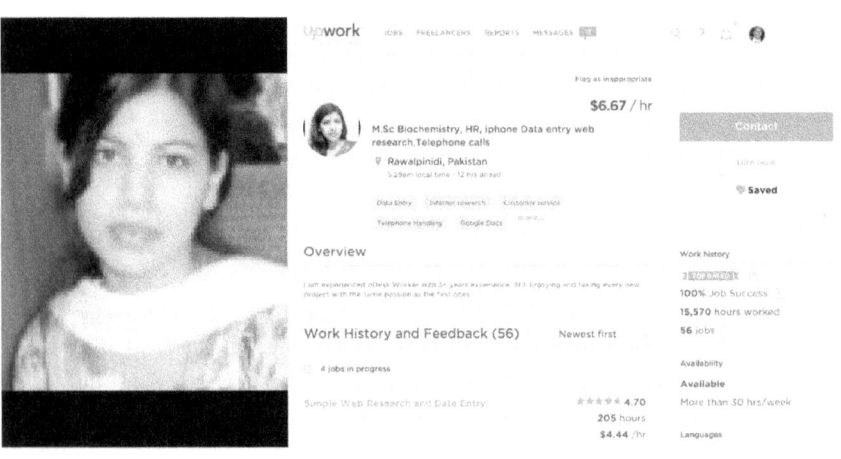

Below is the employment contract that I made with Asmi through Upwork.com. You can see that I spent $2,386.75 on her work. She served as my assistant. In the end, she and I both left each other five stars rating and positive comments. Asmi's future employers can see my positive comments, and these reviews can help employers to understand that she will be very valuable worker and contributor to their teams.

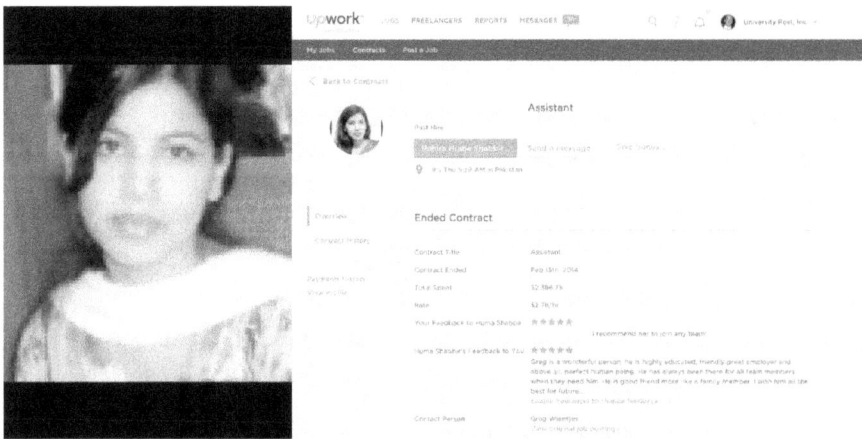

My preference right now in outsourcing is to hire my workers directly and to pay them directly through PayPal. I find that using the mediated payment outsourcing websites can be much more expensive than paying my workers directly. Additionally, the time tracking tools that these mediated outsourcing websites provide can be found using alternative resources such as TimeDoctor or WorkSnaps.com.

As I said, my preference right now is hiring Full-Time Filipinos, and the best source of these workers are found on OnlineJobs.ph. OnlineJobs.ph serves as a resume repository rather than a mediated payment outsourcing website like UpWork. Nevertheless, if OnlineJobs.ph simply does not have the availability of certain types of workers—especially mobile app developers—then I must look into other larger outsourcing websites to find the available "people supply" that I need to accomplish my software projects.

Funnel Hiring In Action

I would like to encapsulate the "Funnel Hiring" process in a specific set of steps that you can replicate in order to achieve success in your recruitment of outsourcing workers. These steps will simplify the process for you to build apps that you envision and to make your dreams a reality.

First, you need to define what you would like to build as best as you can. Ideally, you draw some sketches and make some mockups of the app you envision. This might lead you to writing down a set of skills that your mobile app developer needs to possess. These skills might include, for example, an app's ability to capture a photo—perhaps this app needs to be able to send some text data to the cloud. Once you have these functionalities listed, then you know the types of skills that you need to search for and test within candidates originating from outsourcing websites.

Next, you search for developers that claim to have the skills on the platform that you envision building on first—for example, iOS or android. Post a job on your selected outsourcing websites. Forge ahead by sending out job invitations to a set of a couple hundred developers that claim to have skills on your target mobile platform.

Then, essentially, you hire 100 mobile app developers on some small coding task that is relevant to the app you intend to build. You make this first task very small and quick for competent developers to construct. For example, a competent developer might build this first app or feature in just 15 to 45 minutes. At this point, you can reward the developers that succeeded in building the app with a little bit of money, such as one dollar or $2. You can choose. This is your first performance test.

Funnel Hiring: An Example In Action

- Hire 100 Developers on Same Small Relevant Coding Task
- Performance Tests (Wufoo.com)
- Discover "Geniuses"
- Make Friends with Geniuses!

Then, among the set of developers that pass your first test, you give a second follow-up performance test. Perhaps only 50 developers completed your first test. You pay one dollar to each developer. Now you spent a total of $50.

You give the passed developers the second test, and you perhaps reward those developers that successfully complete the second test with $2 or $3. Suppose only half of those developers pass. You payout $2 to each of the 25 developers that passed—so, that totals $50 again.

Now you give a third follow-up test. Perhaps half of those pass again. Only 12 developers remain. You give each of them $4. Now you're getting to a more manageable level.

Now you have a set of 12 developers that passed three of your tests, and they seem to have the basic skills you need to move forward on your application. At this point, you can choose to test them again with a fourth test and filter them down further. Or, you can invite them to a Skype video chat or perhaps even do a group video chat on GoToMeeting period.

Maybe at this point you want to meet with them and find out more details about their expectations—such as their desires for a monthly or hourly salary. This information gives you further clues about who you might like to hire for completion of the app, and perhaps even a long-term working relationship.

Now you're getting to the point you want to make the offer to hire someone or a set of developers—the "geniuses" you discovered after an extensive testing process. You can say, "You're hired" directly to the candidates on Skype video chat. Or perhaps, you might want to send an email saying, "You're hired". Once I get a candidate to accept the job, I like to have them sign an employment contract—however, those logistics are really up to you. The exciting part is the next phase when you start to collaborate and work with your genius mobile app developers to get your app built.

You've put significant energy into discovering your genius developers; so, you'll want to retain them on your team and perhaps even "make friends". It's actually really fun to video chat with super smart people, living on the other side of the Earth. I promise you'll enjoy it.

Performance Tests

Funnel Hiring

- People Supply
- **Performance Tests**
- Communication & Collaboration

Designing Your Performance Tests: Detailed Mockups

I would like to describe, in more detail, the testing process you perform as part of your recruitment on the outsourcing websites. I like to call this "Performance Tests".

When we design performance tests, we want to make the process as efficient as possible, so that it doesn't take much of our own time to advance candidates forward through our skill testing and selection stages. Imagine sending emails to hundreds of people and answering five or six questions from each person's email one-by-one; this would consume dozens of hours of our time. [40]

In contrast, if we make our test instructions clear and simple, then that will eliminate any need for follow-up questions from candidates. We can speed up the process even faster by "automating" the test submission process through the use of web forms, which I will describe later.

Clarity and simplicity in your Performance Test instructions will save our time. To illustrate further, an effective way to be very clear about what we want built in our performance tests is to construct mockup diagrams—pictures to represent how our mobile app should work. So,

---

[40] Passing a High Jump. https://upload.wikimedia.org/wikipedia/commons/0/0a/High_Jump_Triton_Invitational_2011_2.jpg

candidates, when they look at these diagrams and mockups, they'll know exactly what needs to be built and demonstrated without any questions to us as the employer.

You can see below a mockup of an actual performance test that I constructed for building an application that would allow user to capture a video, save that video on the cloud, and share the video with a friend. Those were the functionalities that I wanted in my desired app. However, for my initial performance tests, I did not test for all of those functionalities all at once. I focused just on the ability to capture a video. I tested for that first, specifically, and then I added more advanced functionality requests in followup tests—such as pushing data to the cloud and sharing videos on social networks.

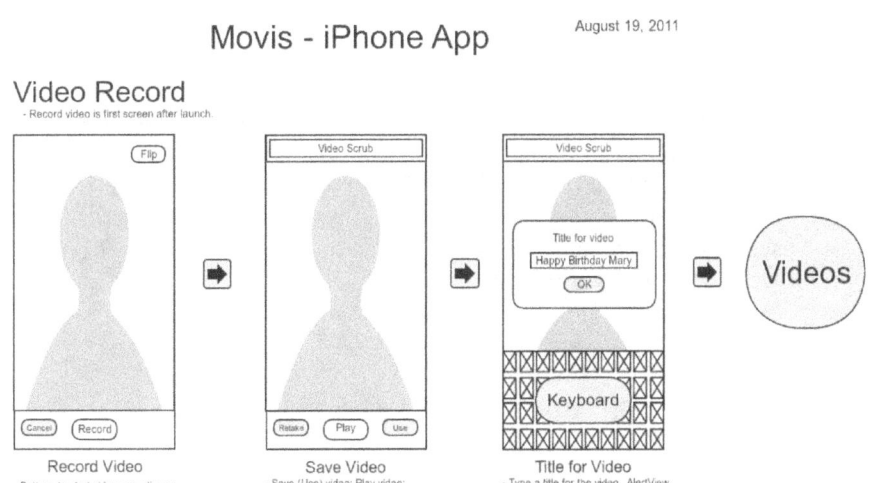

Speed Up Your Testing: Web Forms for Candidates' Submissions

Using web forms to collect candidates' test submissions is another very effective technique to save your own time in testing candidates. In contrast, a novice employer might test candidates by sending emails or receiving submissions through Skype chat. Those types of submissions can be fine if the number of candidates that you're testing are limited. However, if you're testing hundreds of people, you want to use methods that can scale up more efficiently and reduce your time consumption. The solution that I found is using web forms.

My favorite web form to use right now is Wufoo.com. Wufoo will allow you to capture the candidate's name, email, Skype username. Wufoo forms can perform validation of data, ensuring, for example, that the format of an email is correct. Format validated data prevents time wasting submission of "garbage" candidate data. The form can validate that submitted URLs are of correct format. You might like to collect the URL of the candidate's work profile on OnlineJobs.ph or UpWork.com.

The Wufoo web form tool can allow you to collect the performance test submission of the candidate. This submission might take the form of a text area box, containing computer code text. The candidate might submit this block of text as a result of his or her test. The candidate might also upload a file or code project; and, the Wufoo web form tool allows you to upload a file using the upload field. Furthermore, the test submission might take the form of a video link URL, where the candidate demonstrated a functional app that had been screened recorded and uploaded to a video sharing website such as YouTube or Vimeo. The format and modality of the performance tests submission can take on a multitude of representations. Your own imagination will determine what form would be the simplest for the candidates to submit, as well as possess enough validity in the testing process.

Below, you see an example Wufoo submission web form that I used in a Performance Test in finding a mobile app developer on oDesk.com (UpWork.com).

Submission of iPhone Project for Greg

This form is for Odesk iPhone developers to submit their completed XCode projects of the athletics application.

Your Odesk Profile Link *

Email *

Skype Username

Upload Your Completed XCode iPhone Project (zipped) *

Choose File   no file selected

Submit

Rapid Evaluation and Advancement of Candidates — Pass/Fail Tests

The image below shows a screenshot of the "backend" submission review page of candidates' performance tests. We can see a list of candidates that submitted their code. The performance test submission simply involved zipping or compressing the Xcode project which contained the iPhone application code. The code should provide a functional application, and the candidates simply upload a file of their completed functional app project.

Each candidate provided his or her name, as well as email and Skype username. All of this contact information is sufficient to follow-up with candidates and hire them. The submitted application code project is a component in testing their skills.

However, in recent times, I discovered it's actually more efficient to not ask for the completed project—the code itself. Instead, I like to ask the developer candidates to build the application, and then simply make a video screen recording demonstrating the application. This video is enough for me to know if the developer really has the skills I'm looking for. By just watching the video, I don't have to deal with any technical problems with running their applications. I've wasted a lot of time, in the past, trying to get apps to work, while my computer had a different configuration than the app's settings—giving the app problems in running.

Furthermore, the developer oftentimes feels more comfortable first making the screen recording videos and sharing those with me—rather than giving up his or her code. The developer has not yet been paid at the time of the Performance Test submission. Developers oftentimes want to be paid first before they upload and transfer their code and functional application projects.

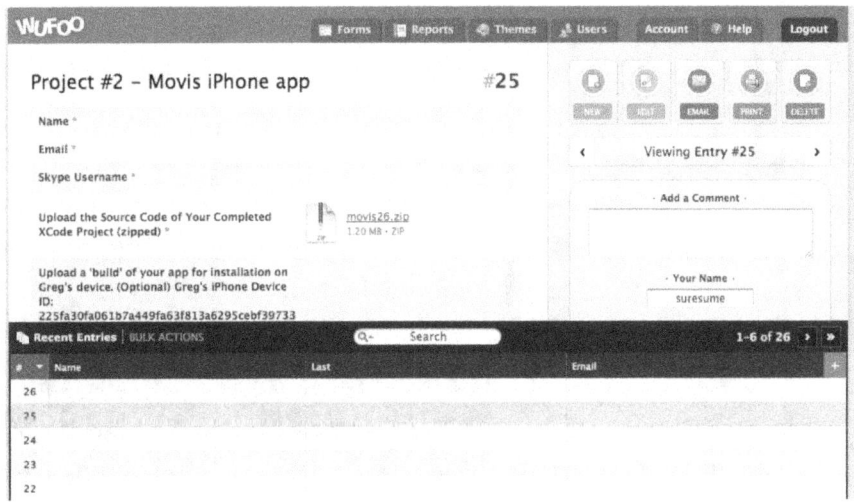

When you look through the submissions, you want to move through them rapidly. You want to be able to look through the submissions and mark them pass or fail quickly, in order to advance the worthy the candidates forward. Only when you get to the end stage of your testing do you want to spend a more extended period of time on any particular individual. At the end of your Performance Tests, your candidates are "filtered down" to a much smaller set of individuals. This has the advantage that there are simply fewer people left at the end of your testing process and less of your time will be consumed to get to know each person more in-depth—perhaps even through a video chat.

Discover the Genius Developer

After you completed your selection process with your performance tests, the next stage is to make offers to hire particular individuals. Ideally, these "survivors" of your testing process are geniuses. Even if they are not geniuses in the global sense, these developers will feel like geniuses to you —because their skills are likely beyond your own skills. So, from your perspective, they really are geniuses.

In the performance test that I described above, I sought to find a mobile app developer able to build an iPhone app for a video-sharing. I ended up finding a very capable mobile app developer that I hired, and he built the application that I envisioned. You can see below the application that we built together: Movis — a video-sharing application like

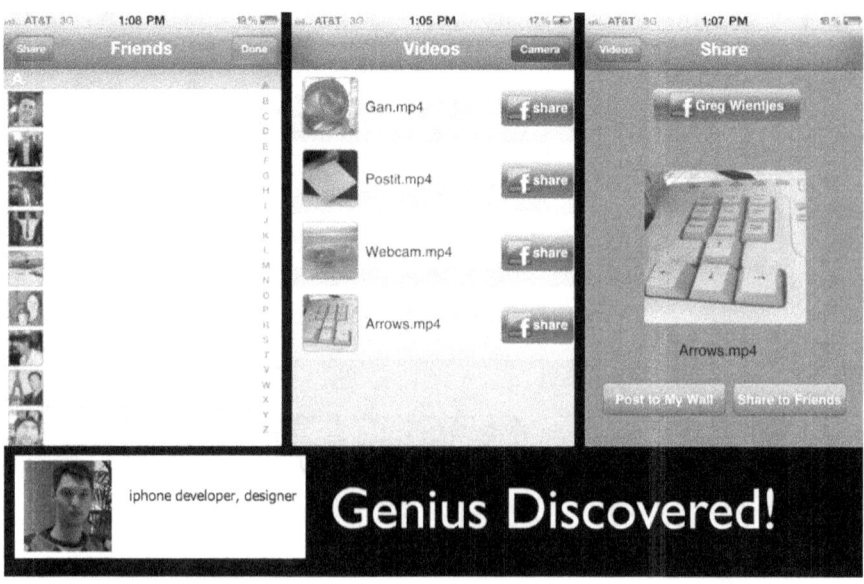

Instagram, but for video. Movis was published live on the App Store. The genius developer that I discovered was based in Russia.

It turns out that Movis was not successful in getting 100 million users or for being sold to Facebook. Good thing that I spent only $500 to get it built—and, I got a chance to try out the idea!

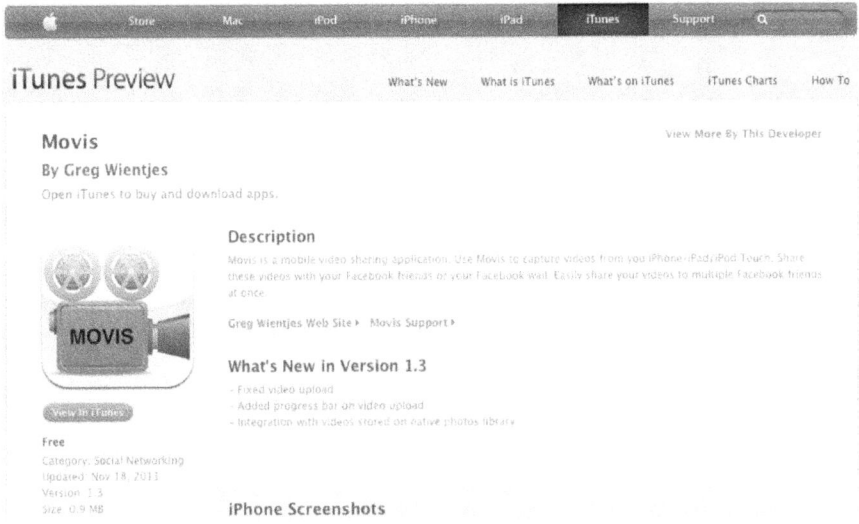

Communication And Collaboration

Funnel Hiring

- People Supply
- Performance Tests
- **Communication & Collaboration**

Skype Video Chat with Your Team

When you find your genius developers—as well as other members of your virtual team and business—you want to work very closely with them. You want to video chat with them a lot on Skype. This type of engaged communication will allow you to understand them and to develop a relationship with them that will make your team and business highly effective.

I spent hundreds of hours video chatting with my team over the years, and the experience has been great. Your virtual team becomes a social support group for you, as well as to members of the team. These video chat conversations allow you to understand what factors are going on in the lives of your workers—and you can use this information to help them in their lives and also to help guide the team towards productive business goals.

The video chat screenshot below was taken together with me and three of my workers. The two people on the left side worked for me for over a year now. You can see me down at the bottom, working out of my bedroom and wearing a wireless headset. Each of the team members are

also effective working out of the bedrooms in their homes in the Philippines.

This next image shows a "virtual birthday party" that my team held for me on my birthday. You can see Kate—in the center—presenting a birthday cake to me. The team together sang the "happy birthday" song to me. Meanwhile, Kate lit a candle on the cake. When the song finished, I blew into the web camera, and Kate assisted me by blowing out the candle on her side in Manila, Philippines.

This "virtual birthday party" gives you a sense of the rapport and togetherness that the team members feel with each other. This unity and emotional connection serves multiple purposes, including making the work experience more enjoyable for everybody, as well as improving the richness and depth of communication for business problem-solving purposes on the team. All of this communication and emotional connection combines together to create a "synergy" that leads to higher productivity, better results, more sales, more revenue and more excitement and fun.

Create a "Hive Mind" Team Using Slack Messaging

I discovered, in the last few months, a new tool that really improved the communication and collaboration among my team members: Slack, a messaging software.

Slack serves a purpose similar to Skype in that it allows team members to send messages to each other. However, an advantage is that, when a new member of the team gets added to the group, that new member instantly has access to all of the members on the team. On Skype, in contrast, a new member of the team must "add as a contact" everybody on the team. You can imagine that, if the team size exceeds 10 people or even 100 people, such a task is time consuming and needlessly complicated.

On Slack, once a new teammate is added to the group, he or she can see the detailed profiles of each person on the team, and these details might include a cell phone number, email, Skype username. The image sharing features of Slack make conversations more information rich. Plus, I just love the Slack iPhone application, because communication among team members is so fast for sending out messages—both to individuals and to groups of team members through the use of #channels.

The increased efficiency and communication enabled by the Slack messaging application creates a sense of a "hive mind", as if the team is a single individual operating in unity. A "hive mind" team operates smoothly and effectively in executing objectives—achieving far more than individuals acting independently typically could accomplish. This enhancement in team dynamics represents a "level up" from my previous experiences using Skype.

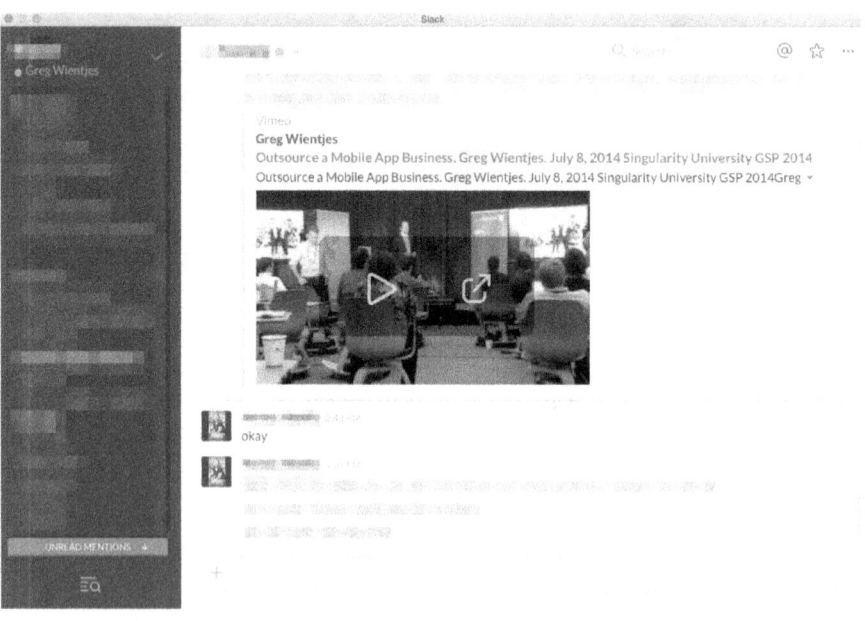

Regular Meetings with GoToMeeting and 'Synergy Reports'

I learned, in working with my virtual team, that a helpful practice is to have regular "team meetings" on video chat as a group. Doing these team meetings three times per week keeps up a strong momentum. If a long time goes by without you closely communicating with the team, then things can really go wrong. People start to get consumed in their own lives and focused on their own personal circumstances. However, in contrast, when you have regular team meetings three times per week, that gives a chance for people to get focused on the team goals again and work through communication problems. Below shows a team meeting that we held on GoToMeeting. Asmi, who you met in a previous worker profile image on UpWork.com/oDesk.com, is shown on the top right—while I am in the center top of the image.

In the photo below, during one of our team meetings, we are holding another "virtual birthday party". This photo was taken on a prior year to the "virtual birthday party" held in the image displayed earlier in this book.

Additionally, I discovered that daily reports and communication from individual teammates to me personally help keep the team on track—I call these daily communications "synergy reports". In these synergy reports, I ask my teammates to answer three questions. In fact, these questions originated from the trainings offered from John Jonas's Udemy lecture videos on how to work with a team of Filipino outsourcing teammates. The three questions that I ask my teammates to answer in their synergy reports are the following:

- What did you work on today?
- What problems or challenges did you experience today in your work?
- How can Greg help you with your work?

The synergy reports need to also include the name of the teammate, his or her email, and the number of hours worked in that day.

In the past, I asked for the synergy reports to be simply sent as a Skype message to me daily. However, lately, I find it helpful to ask teammates to submit their synergy reports both through a Wufoo.com form —to keep a record—and then also send them to me individually as a Slack or Skype message. When you get these daily synergy reports, you can relax—and not feel the need to "micro-manage"—because you know the teammates are really working towards business goals.

Visiting Your Team Physically In Their Country

If you ever get a chance to go visit your virtual team in person, go do it. It's really an amazing experience to meet your virtual team in person.

After working with a set of Full-Time Filipinos for over six months, I decided, in October 2014, to fly to Manila and meet some of them in person. You can see six of us below. Five of my outsourcing workers greeted me at the airport in Manila and took me to a restaurant for dinner. We had a really nice time talking in person, getting to know each other on a deeper level.

When you meet your outsourcing teammates in person, you have an even stronger sense of emotional connection. Once you make that emotional connection, you can take it with you even when you're back at home and maintain that healthy sense of trust and rapport. Personally, I like to fly to the Philippines at least once a year to meet my virtual team. I might even start doing it more frequently in the near future, such as twice per year.

On my trip to the Philippines in 2014, we decided to take a reward vacation together to Subic Bay—two hours north of Manila. In Subic Bay, we went swimming with dolphins. The experience was really an adventure, and doing it together with my virtual team was quite a thrill. In fact, going swimming with dolphins was on my "bucket list" and experiencing it together with my team really still does give me a smile when I think about it almost a year since that time. In the center, you see me holding the dolphin that we were assigned to swim with. Behind me is Kate—who you met earlier in some of the synergy team meetings. She lives in a suburb of Manila, and we brought her husband, sisters, brother and mom with us to this beach outing.

EXAMPLE   60

Example

Building a Mobile App For My Marketplace Business

I would like to "flesh out" further the process to outsource your mobile app business by presenting a specific example—when I developed a mobile app interface for my marketplace website dedicated to university campuses. My website consists of a listing of advertisements posted by university students. Students submit these advertisements online through a web form—by clicking the post link at the top right corner of the webpage. Additionally, the advertisement data is classified based on categories, including for sale, personals, housing, jobs, campus jobs, community and services.

After a few years operating purely a website business, I learned that over 70% of the student users had iPhones. I felt that the mobile app interface would be very useful as a supplement to the website. So, I set out to construct an iPhone app interface for my website!

Mockup Sketches of My Envisioned Mobile App Using GoMockingbird

Once I set the goal to build a mobile app for my business, I developed my initial ideas about how the app should work by drawing sketches on a piece of paper. These sketches helped me to understand the core functionalities needed for the app. Examples of such functionalities included: (1) the ability to view a set of posts, (2) the ability to respond to a post and send an email, and (3) the ability to submit a post.

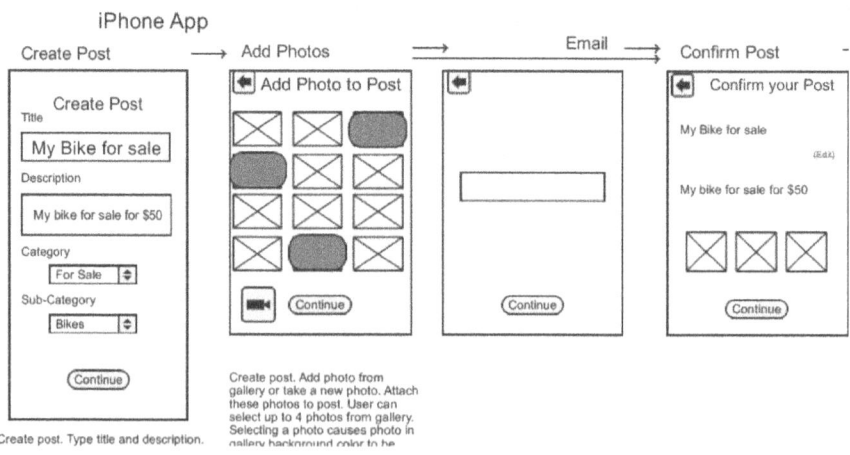

EXAMPLE   62

Next, I decided to build a sketch of the app that I am envisioned on my computer. I used the tool called GoMockingbird.com, which is a website to allow you to quickly drag different shapes and components into a canvas to get a rough idea of how app might work.

An advantage of using a computer tool to draw sketches is that you can make changes seamlessly between your designs and not have to redraw your sketches by hand. With your designs online, you can collaboratively develop your sketches through a cloud-based web interface together with users or even software developers. This type of mockup online can be very helpful for creating iterations in your design, as well as sharing your prototypes with other people quickly. Of course, you can also print out these designs and show them to potential users and friends in person and get their rapid feedback. Check out one of my sketches below for my mobile app that I built using GoMockingbird.

Simulating Your App Using AppCooker

As a next step in constructing the design for my mobile app, I moved ahead towards building mockups of what the app should look like using a "simulation" mockup tool called AppCooker—together with its companion software, AppTaster. An advantage of using a "simulation" mockup tool is that you can "wire together" components of your application. These linkages between screens of your mockup allow you or users to "try out" your application screens, buttons and components—in a way that simulates a functional application. You can "hyperlink" buttons together, so that pressing a particular button will allow the user to advance forward to the appropriate next screen. For example, hyperlinking a "post" button might advance the user to the "data posting" screen.

No coding is required for you to build such a simulation application. You can even show the simulation to users and potential customers and get their feedback already without any time or development expense invested.

Furthermore, these simulations give very clear instructions to your developers, saving you and your developer time and reducing the back-and-forth communication needed to implement the mobile app.

Below is a screenshot of AppCooker on the App Store, where you can download it for your iPad. You can create detailed mockups of your envisioned mobile app on this iPad application. Once you have your app constructed, you can distribute it out to other devices such as the iPhone using a free companion application called AppTaster.

The following image is the search results listing page that I envisioned for my mobile application. Notice the blue rectangle covering one of the search result listings. This blue rectangle is a clickable link to

EXAMPLE   64

allow a user testing the application to advance to the next screen on the simulation mockup. These hyperlinks are extremely useful for testing out different user interfaces before any actual coding gets done.

Imagine that you are building a house. You don't want to cut the wood used to construct the house with the wrong measurements. You would be wise to "measure twice and cut once". This analogy applies to building software. Better to develop different versions of the design of your app using a mockup tool and get confident that users will find your app helpful ("measure") and then send a clear instruction to your developer for implementation ("cut").

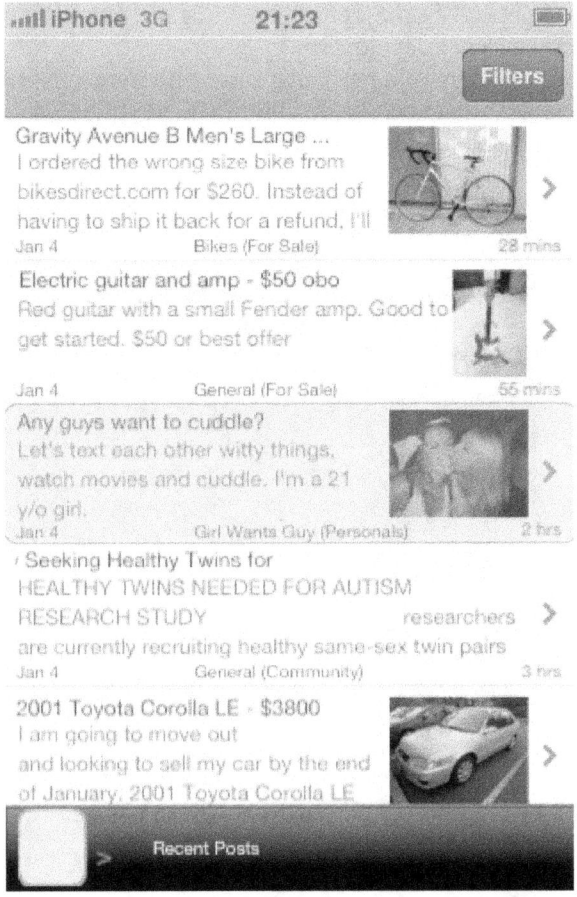

Of course, you will need to make changes to your app based on user feedback. However, the fewer changes you make, the easier it will be on your developers to build the app rapidly and cost efficiently. Simulating your application using AppCooker will allow you to get user feedback even before you build any actual code. When your users give you the "green light" that your application is useful and the user interface makes sense to them, you will be much more confident when you get your app implemented.

Furthermore, the simulation app gives very clear instructions about what the application functionality and user interface should be to your developer. If you simply make mockup sketches without the simulated page links wired together, developers may have much more uncertainty about how the application should work. This uncertainty will cause you to have additional conversations and will delay the construction of your mobile application. Thus, building the simulated application on AppCooker will speed up your time to development of your app, making the construction of your app cheaper and the process more enjoyable for both you and your developers.

A mockup of a particular post reply screen is depicted below. "Placeholder" text is contained within the text fields to give an idea about how this component of the application works. The user of this simulated

EXAMPLE   66

mockup app would just simply click on the blue rectangle text area in order to advance the app forward to a new screen to see how the "user flow" behaves.

'Storyboard' Screens of Your App Using AppCooker

A "storyboard", in the image below, shows how the mobile app screens are "wired together". The blue rectangle hyperlinks in the individual application screens are the "connection points" for the user to navigate between the various mockup pages. Notice that the screens—connected together on the storyboard—form a closed loop so that the user can navigate among the screens and not get stuck at a dead end. A user testing out this simulated mockup of the application can seamlessly visit each of the mobile app screens and get a sense for how the application would work—clicking blue rectangles repeatedly on the screens in order to advance forward.

Recall also that no computer programming is needed to develop this mobile app simulation. You can really get a good sense of how the application will work just simply based on these mockup screens. Not only that, you can show actual users your application and get their

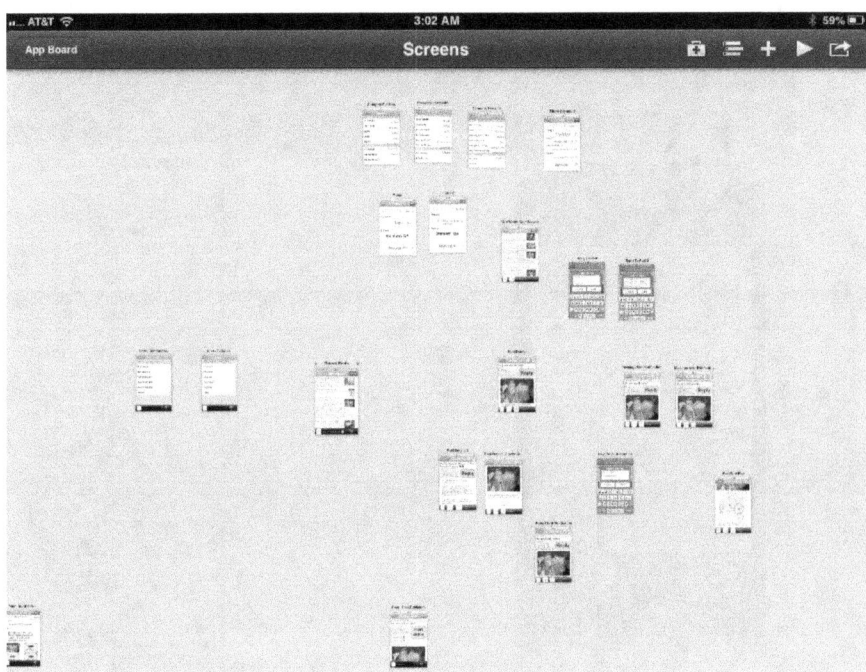

feedback immediately—without waiting for any developer to actually construct your application. This is a massive time savings. You might discover that the application that you envision isn't even useful or helpful at all for users. A simulated app will help you get that feedback right away, before you spend any time or money on constructing the application. In that situation, you could "move on" to a new app idea without wasting time or money.

Creation Tools for Your Simulated App Using AppCooker

The following screen shows AppCooker's creation tool used to build your "simulated" mockup. You drag and drop buttons and app components onto a main canvas screen. You build up your application screen one-by-one, button-by-button, image-by-image.

A major advantage of using an app prototyping tool such as AppCooker is that it prevents you from being too "perfectionistic" about your application mockups at this stage. In the early stages of building your application, you don't want to spend an excessive number of hours fine-tuning button colors, placement of text on the page, and color schemes; these details might never be incorporated in the final live application or even matter at all.

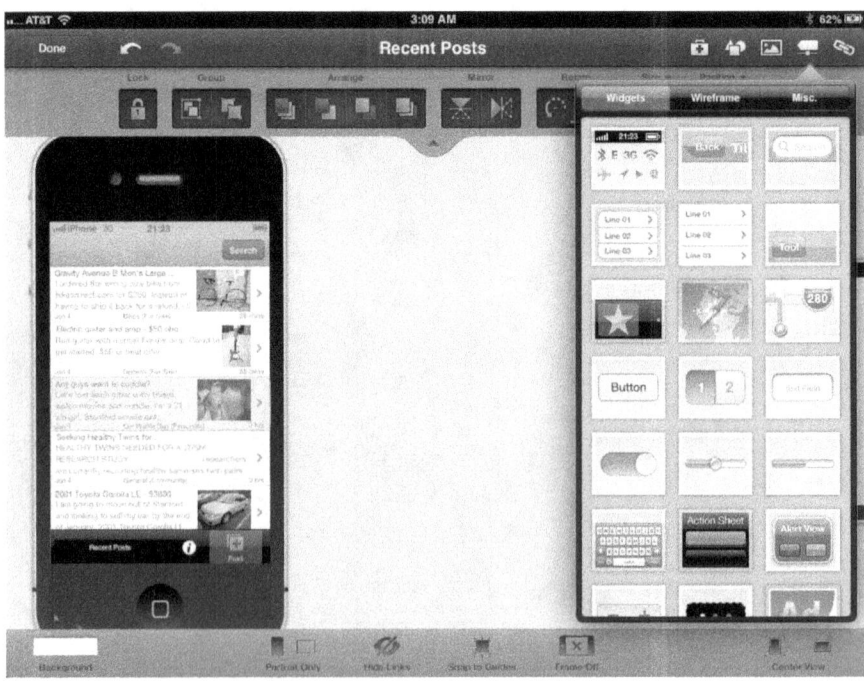

EXAMPLE   68

In the early stages of creating a mobile app, you want to prototype basic functionalities—create a minimum viable product—just something working that you can show your target users and customers in order to get their feedback about whether they find it actually valuable, and perhaps even something they might be willing to pay for. Build just the minimum set of functionalities in your product needed to get the idea across to your target users and customers. 10 hours of your time is better spent with a roughly simulated mockup prototype in your hands showing it to actual users and having conversations about their reactions, than spending 10 hours fine-tuning text and image placement on a hypothetical prototype that only you've seen.

A Functional App

Depicted below is the functional application that my mobile app developer created once I provided him with the mockups from GoMockingbird and AppCooker. You can see that the functional mobile app screens below align very closely with the screens that I developed for the prototype on AppCooker. I updated the AppCooker screens repeatedly as we developed our ideas and got feedback from potential users. Thus, the AppCooker screens served as a type of sandbox for me to continually mold iteratively and reimagine based on what we had learned so far in our development.

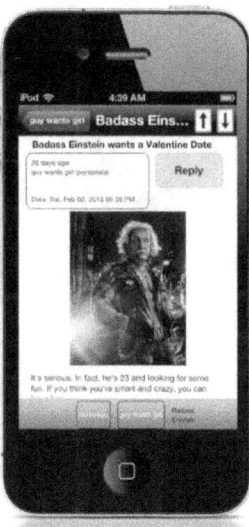

My Genius Developer: Amdad

The genius developer that I discovered—through my Performance Tests—to help me build my mobile application for my website business was: Amdad. You can see him in the below photo. Amdad comes from Bangladesh, and I found him on the website UpWork.com. In order to find Amdad, I considered 500+ developers; I posted a job; I sent out job invitations to 200+ developers; I received 35 submissions of iPhone app tests. Just by looking at these numbers you can see "Funnel Hiring" in action.

I spent a total of $435 to get the mobile application built for my business—this amount included fees I paid to the 35 tested developers and the total payment sum that I gave to Amdad.

My working relationship with Amdad carries on even to this day. He made even more income from me through follow-up projects on other apps that we developed. Amdad has a portfolio of clients that he assists and receives income from—allowing him to support himself, his wife, his baby and his mother in Bangladesh living with him.

Summary Of Resources

People Supply

     This chart shows a set of websites to help you find and recruit outsourcing workers, including mobile app developers. As I said before, my favorite approach right now is to hire Full-Time Filipinos. The best place to hire Full-Time Filipinos is through OnlineJobs.ph. An alternative place to find Filipinos includes BestJobs.ph, as well as searching by country on UpWork.com and Elance.com.

     For mobile app developers, you really need to recruit from a wider set of available people then exclusively Filipinos. You need to consider places like India, Pakistan, China, Vietnam and Eastern Europe. So, I look at recruiting mobile app developers from UpWork.com. However, you can also take a look at some of the other outsourcing websites shown in the chart below.

People Supply

Full-Time Filipinos:

OnlineJobs.ph
BestJobs.ph

More Outsourcing Sites:

UpWork.com	Craigslist.com	99designs
Elance.com	GetACoder	Amazon Mechanical Turk
Guru.com	iFreelance	PeoplePerHour
Freelancer.com	SimplyHired	Twago.com

Tools for Your Outsourcing

I also would like to outline some of the tools that I found helpful in my outsourcing work in the chart below. These are resources to help you streamline your recruiting process, make your evaluation and selection process efficient and enable information rich and rapid online collaborations with your remote team.

A helpful resource to consider if you would like to learn more is John Jonas' Udemy course, "How to Hire Talented Virtual Assistants From the Philippines". I also love Tim Ferriss' "Four Hour Work Week", which first open my eyes to the potential and productivity associated with outsourcing. Furthermore, Eric Ries' book, "Lean Startup", is a highly effective approach to developing software in a fun and cost efficient way.

Tools

Performance Tests	Wufoo.com, Google Doc Forms, Max BulkMailer, SendGrid.com / MailJet SMTP
Collaboration	Skype, GoToMeeting, Slack, Skitch, Jing (TechSmith), Asana.com, BitBucket.org, GitHub.com
Writing Specs	AppCooker, Hackpad.com, Google Docs, LucidChart.com, GoMockingbird.com
Strategy	John Jonas (How To Hire Talented Virtual Assistants From The Philippines; Udemy Video) Tim Ferriss (Four Hour Work Week) Eric Ries (Lean StartUp)

You Can Do It

For my doctoral dissertation at Stanford University, I studied geniuses in technology. These geniuses included the "Fathers of the Internet", Vint Cerf and Bob Kahn. The geniuses included winners of the Nobel Prize and National Medal of Science award.

In my study, I discovered a number of key conditions and habits that helped to create circumstances for the geniuses to be able to express their inherent creative capabilities and achieve technology inventions and breakthroughs to an extraordinary extent. A major finding was that these geniuses had mentors that told them: "You can do it".

The geniuses had people that believed in them and their creative capabilities. Their mentors saw in them a power and strength within that lay dormant and needed just a little extra push to make that the creative spirit come out of their hearts and minds and shine for the world.

Singularity University launched us out into the world with the hopes that we can help solve the world's Grand Challenges and help improve the lives of 1 billion+ people. Now, it's your turn! You are a member of the next class of GSP students!

Today, I would like to be that mentor for you. I give you a call to action. You can do it. You can make your dreams reality. You can collect your creative inner ideas and organize them in a way that is achievable and implementable. Your imagination and visions are just waiting to come out and help the world. Use your hands and ideas—as well as resources and skills—to make it happen. You can do it!

Sincerely,
Greg Wientjes, PhD
Stanford, California. July 12, 2015

Acknowledgements

To my Mom and Dad, Suzanne and Brent Wientjes,
who gave me a "safety net" of support after completing my PhD at
Stanford,
who gave me first life in November of 1980,
who nurtured and protected me throughout all of my years,
who inspire and encourage me to 'do my best',
who provided the foundation for me to be all that I can be,
who compel me to want to 'give back' and help other people as part
of the unconditional love I received from you both,
who valued education and the university so much,
who 'stick together' despite hardship,
who help me to see my potential,
who I love very much and feel so grateful for.

Thank you very much, Mom and Dad, for your love and support and
everything you've done for me throughout my life.

Thank you to Brad Templeton and David Roberts, for inviting me to
speak to the GSP students at Singularity University on the topic of
outsourcing a mobile app business.

Thank you to Ray Kurzweil and Peter Diamandis for founding
Singularity University and admitting me as a GSP student in 2009.

Thank you to Stan Wanat for encouraging to write this book and for
helping me to develop my thoughts about the ethics of this topic.

Thank you to my "virtual team" and to the hundreds more that hired.

About the Author

Greg Wientjes, Ph.D., was awarded his Stanford doctoral degree (Developmental and Psychological Sciences) in 2010. Wientjes attended Singularity University (2009), and authored the book, Creative Genius in Technology, http://amzn.com/146372750X

Dr. Wientjes completed his Master's of Science in Electrical Engineering (2006) and his Bachelor of Science degree in Mathematics (2004), both from Stanford.

Dr. Wientjes learned outsourcing techniques through personal experience hiring developers and business process workers on remote employment networks such as oDesk.com, UpWork.com, and OnlineJobs.ph. Wientjes hired these outsource workers as a part of developing a startup business—both a website and mobile app —and this business served as a marketplace for university students.

Published in North America by CreateSpace Independent Publishing Platform,
www.createspace.com, print division. Materials such as images contained are
copyright to Greg Wientjes, unless referenced to another source. Some images
contain originate from the Bing Image Search and Google Image Search and were
labeled as with a Creative Commons License with permission for reuse. Cover
photo of Earth contained was available as Creative Commons via NASA.

Library of Congress Cataloging-In-Publication Data

Wientjes, Greg.
     Outsource Your Mobile App Business: Ethics and Pragmatics of Hiring
          Genius Software Developers Worldwide.
     ISBN-13: 978-1515393603
     ISBN-10: 1515393607
     Printed In The United States of America

www.ingramcontent.com/pod-product-compliance
Lightning Source LLC
Chambersburg PA
CBHW070835180526
45168CB00002B/843